Select

~

Selected Poems

W.B. Yeats

Selected by

J.G. Nichols

ALMA CLASSICS

ALMA CLASSICS LTD
Hogarth House
32-34 Paradise Road
Richmond
Surrey TW9 1SE
United Kingdom
www.almaclassics.com

First published by Alma Classics Ltd (previously Oneworld Classics Ltd)
in 2010.
This new edition first published by Alma Classics Ltd in 2015
Extra Material © J.G. Nichols, 2010
Front-cover image © Kay Maguire Photography

Printed in Great Britain by CPI Group (UK) Ltd, Croydon CR0 4YY

ISBN: 978-1-84749-441-2

Contents

Selected Poems

The Song of the Happy Shepherd

The woods of Arcady are dead,
And over is their antique joy;
Of old the world on dreaming fed;
Grey Truth is now her painted toy;
Yet still she turns her restless head:
But O, sick children of the world,
Of all the many changing things
In dreary dancing past us whirled,
To the cracked tune that Chronos* sings,
Words alone are certain good.   10
Where are now the warring kings,
Word be-mockers? – By the Rood,
Where are now the warring kings?
An idle word is now their glory,
By the stammering schoolboy said,
Reading some entangled story:
The kings of the old time are dead;
The wandering earth herself may be
Only a sudden flaming word,
In clanging space a moment heard,   20
Troubling the endless reverie.
Then nowise worship dusty deeds,
Nor seek, for this is also sooth,
To hunger fiercely after truth,
Lest all thy toiling only breeds
New dreams, new dreams; there is no truth
Saving in thine own heart. Seek, then,
No learning from the starry men,
Who follow with the optic glass
The whirling ways of stars that pass –   30
Seek, then, for this is also sooth,
No word of theirs – the cold star-bane
Has cloven and rent their hearts in twain,
And dead is all their human truth.

Go gather by the humming sea
Some twisted, echo-harbouring shell,
And to its lips thy story tell,
And they thy comforters will be,
Rewording in melodious guile
Thy fretful words a little while,   40
Till they shall singing fade in ruth
And die a pearly brotherhood;
For words alone are certain good:
Sing, then, for this is also sooth.

I must be gone: there is a grave
Where daffodil and lily wave,
And I would please the hapless faun,
Buried under the sleepy ground,
With mirthful songs before the dawn.
His shouting days with mirth were crowned;   50
And still I dream he treads the lawn,
Walking ghostly in the dew,
Pierced by my glad singing through,
My songs of old earth's dreamy youth:
But ah! she dreams not now; dream thou!
For fair are poppies on the brow:
Dream, dream, for this is also sooth.

Down by the Salley Gardens

Down by the salley gardens my love and I did meet;
She passed the salley gardens with little snow-white feet.
She bid me take love easy, as the leaves grow on the tree;
But I, being young and foolish, with her would not agree.

In a field by the river my love and I did stand,
And on my leaning shoulder she laid her snow-white hand.
She bid me take life easy, as the grass grows on the weirs;
But I was young and foolish, and now am full of tears.

The Meditation of the Old Fisherman

You waves, though you dance by my feet like children at play,
Though you glow and you glance, though you purr and you dart;
In the Junes that were warmer than these are, the waves were more gay,
When I was a boy with never a crack in my heart.

The herring are not in the tides as they were of old;
My sorrow! for many a creak gave the creel in the cart
That carried the take to Sligo town to be sold,
When I was a boy with never a crack in my heart.

And ah, you proud maiden, you are not so fair when his oar
Is heard on the water, as they were, the proud and apart,   10
Who paced in the eve by the nets on the pebbly shore,
When I was a boy with never a crack in my heart.

Cuchulain's Fight with the Sea

A man came slowly from the setting sun,
To Emer, raddling raiment in her dun,
And said, "I am that swineherd whom you bid
Go watch the road between the wood and tide,
But now I have no need to watch it more."

Then Emer cast the web upon the floor,
And raising arms all raddled with the dye,
Parted her lips with a loud sudden cry.

That swineherd stared upon her face and said,
"No man alive, no man among the dead,   10
Has won the gold his cars of battle bring."

"But if your master comes home triumphing
Why must you blench and shake from foot to crown?"

Thereon he shook the more and cast him down
Upon the web-heaped floor, and cried his word:
"With him is one sweet-throated like a bird."

"You dare me to my face," and thereupon
She smote with raddled fist, and where her son
Herded the cattle came with stumbling feet,
And cried with angry voice, "It is not meet   20
To idle life away, a common herd."

"I have long waited, mother, for that word:
But wherefore now?"

               "There is a man to die;
You have the heaviest arm under the sky."

"Whether under its daylight or its stars
My father stands amid his battle-cars."

"But you have grown to be the taller man."

"Yet somewhere under starlight or the sun
My father stands."

              "Aged, worn out with wars
On foot, on horseback or in battle-cars."   30

"I only ask what way my journey lies,
For He who made you bitter made you wise."

"The Red Branch camp in a great company
Between wood's rim and the horses of the sea.
Go there, and light a camp-fire at wood's rim;
But tell your name and lineage to him
Whose blade compels, and wait till they have found
Some feasting man that the same oath has bound."

Among those feasting men Cuchulain dwelt,
And his young sweetheart close beside him knelt,   40
Stared on the mournful wonder of his eyes,
Even as Spring upon the ancient skies,
And pondered on the glory of his days;
And all around the harp-string told his praise,
And Conchubar, the Red Branch king of kings,
With his own fingers touched the brazen strings.
At last Cuchulain spake, "Some man has made
His evening fire amid the leafy shade.
I have often heard him singing to and fro,
I have often heard the sweet sound of his bow.   50
Seek out what man he is."

                  One went and came.
"He bade me let all know he gives his name
At the sword-point, and waits till we have found
Some feasting man that the same oath has bound."

Cuchulain cried, "I am the only man
Of all this host so bound from childhood on."

After short fighting in the leafy shade,
He spake to the young man, "Is there no maid
Who loves you, no white arms to wrap you round,
Or do you long for the dim sleepy ground,   60
That you have come and dared me to my face?"

"The dooms of men are in God's hidden place."

"Your head a while seemed like a woman's head
That I loved once."

                Again the fighting sped,
But now the war-rage in Cuchulain woke,
And through that new blade's guard the old blade broke,
And pierced him.

               "Speak before your breath is done."

"Cuchulain I, mighty Cuchulain's son."

"I put you from your pain. I can no more."

While day its burden on to evening bore,   70
With head bowed on his knees Cuchulain stayed;
Then Conchubar sent that sweet-throated maid,
And she, to win him, his grey hair caressed;
In vain her arms, in vain her soft white breast.
Then Conchubar, the subtlest of all men,
Ranking his Druids round him ten by ten,
Spake thus: "Cuchulain will dwell there and brood
For three days more in dreadful quietude,
And then arise, and raving slay us all.
Chaunt in his ear delusions magical,   80
That he may fight the horses of the sea."
The Druids took them to their mystery,
And chaunted for three days.
                    Cuchulain stirred,
Stared on the horses of the sea, and heard
The cars of battle and his own name cried;
And fought with the invulnerable tide.

When You Are Old

When you are old and grey and full of sleep,
And nodding by the fire, take down this book,
And slowly read, and dream of the soft look
Your eyes had once, and of their shadows deep;

How many loved your moments of glad grace,
And loved your beauty with love false or true,
But one man loved the pilgrim soul in you,
And loved the sorrows of your changing face;

And bending down beside the glowing bars,
Murmur, a little sadly, how Love fled   10
And paced upon the mountains overhead
And hid his face amid a crowd of stars.

The Lamentation of the Old Pensioner

Although I shelter from the rain
Under a broken tree,
My chair was nearest to the fire
In every company
That talked of love or politics,
Ere Time transfigured me.

Though lads are making pikes again
For some conspiracy,
And crazy rascals rage their fill
At human tyranny;   10
My contemplations are of Time
That has transfigured me.

There's not a woman turns her face
Upon a broken tree,
And yet the beauties that I loved
Are in my memory;
I spit into the face of Time
That has transfigured me.

He Wishes for the Cloths of Heaven

Had I the heavens' embroidered cloths,
Enwrought with golden and silver light,
The blue and the dim and the dark cloths
Of night and light and the half-light,
I would spread the cloths under your feet:
But I, being poor, have only my dreams;
I have spread my dreams under your feet;
Tread softly because you tread on my dreams.

Never Give All the Heart

Never give all the heart, for love
Will hardly seem worth thinking of
To passionate women if it seem
Certain, and they never dream
That it fades out from kiss to kiss;
For everything that's lovely is
But a brief, dreamy, kind delight.
O never give the heart outright,
For they, for all smooth lips can say,
Have given their hearts up to the play.   10
And who could play it well enough
If deaf and dumb and blind with love?
He that made this knows all the cost,
For he gave all his heart and lost.

Adam's Curse

We sat together at one summer's end,
That beautiful mild woman, your close friend,
And you and I, and talked of poetry.
I said, "A line will take us hours maybe;
Yet if it does not seem a moment's thought,
Our stitching and unstitching has been naught.
Better go down upon your marrow-bones
And scrub a kitchen pavement, or break stones
Like an old pauper, in all kinds of weather;
For to articulate sweet sounds together   10
Is to work harder than all these, and yet
Be thought an idler by the noisy set
Of bankers, schoolmasters and clergymen
The martyrs call the world."

                     And thereupon
That beautiful mild woman for whose sake
There's many a one shall find out all heartache
On finding that her voice is sweet and low
Replied, "To be born woman is to know –
Although they do not talk of it at school –
That we must labour to be beautiful."   20

I said, "It's certain there is no fine thing
Since Adam's fall but needs much labouring.
There have been lovers who thought love should be
So much compounded of high courtesy
That they would sigh and quote with learned looks
Precedents out of beautiful old books;
Yet now it seems an idle trade enough."

We sat grown quiet at the name of love;
We saw the last embers of daylight die,
And in the trembling blue-green of the sky   30

A moon, worn as if it had been a shell
Washed by time's waters as they rose and fell
About the stars and broke in days and years.

I had a thought for no one's but your ears:
That you were beautiful, and that I strove
To love you in the old high way of love;
That it had all seemed happy, and yet we'd grown
As weary-hearted as that hollow moon.

The Old Men Admiring Themselves in the Water

I heard the old, old men say,
"Everything alters,
And one by one we drop away."
They had hands like claws, and their knees
Were twisted like the old thorn-trees
By the waters.
I heard the old, old men say,
"All that's beautiful drifts away
Like the waters."

Words

I had this thought a while ago,
"My darling cannot understand
What I have done, or what would do
In this blind bitter land."

And I grew weary of the sun
Until my thoughts cleared up again,
Remembering that the best I have done
Was done to make it plain;

That every year I have cried, "At length
My darling understands it all,   10
Because I have come into my strength,
And words obey my call";

That had she done so who can say
What would have shaken from the sieve?
I might have thrown poor words away
And been content to live.

Peace

Ah, that Time could touch a form
That could show what Homer's age
Bred to be a hero's wage.
"Were not all her life but storm
Would not painters paint a form
Of such noble lines," I said,
"Such a delicate high head,
All that sternness amid charm,
All that sweetness amid strength?"
Ah, but peace that comes at length,   10
Came when Time had touched her form.

The Fascination of What's Difficult

The fascination of what's difficult
Has dried the sap out of my veins, and rent
Spontaneous joy and natural content
Out of my heart. There's something ails our colt
That must, as if it had not holy blood
Nor on Olympus leaped from cloud to cloud,
Shiver under the lash, strain, sweat and jolt
As though it dragged road metal. My curse on plays
That have to be set up in fifty ways,
On the day's war with every knave and dolt,   10
Theatre business, management of men.
I swear before the dawn comes round again
I'll find the stable and pull out the bolt.

Upon a House Shaken by the Land Agitation

How should the world be luckier if this house,
Where passion and precision have been one
Time out of mind, became too ruinous
To breed the lidless eye that loves the sun?
And the sweet laughing eagle thoughts that grow
Where wings have memory of wings, and all
That comes of the best knit to the best? Although
Mean roof-trees were the sturdier for its fall,
How should their luck run high enough to reach
The gifts that govern men, and after these   10
To gradual Time's last gift, a written speech
Wrought of high laughter, loveliness and ease?

These Are the Clouds

These are the clouds about the fallen sun,
The majesty that shuts his burning eye:
The weak lay hand on what the strong has done,
Till that be tumbled that was lifted high
And discord follow upon unison,
And all things at one common level lie.
And therefore, friend, if your great race were run
And these things came, so much the more thereby
Have you made greatness your companion,
Although it be for children that you sigh: 10
These are the clouds about the fallen sun,
The majesty that shuts his burning eye.

At Galway Races

There where the course is,
Delight makes all of the one mind,
The riders upon the galloping horses,
The crowd that closes in behind:
We, too, had good attendance once,
Hearers and hearteners of the work;
Ay, horsemen for companions,
Before the merchant and the clerk
Breathed on the world with timid breath.
Sing on: somewhere at some new moon,   10
We'll learn that sleeping is not death,
Hearing the whole earth change its tune,
Its flesh being wild, and it again
Crying aloud as the racecourse is,
And we find hearteners among men
That ride upon horses.

All Things Can Tempt Me

All things can tempt me from this craft of verse:
One time it was a woman's face, or worse –
The seeming needs of my fool-driven land;
Now nothing but comes readier to the hand
Than this accustomed toil. When I was young,
I had not given a penny for a song
Did not the poet sing it with such airs
That one believed he had a sword upstairs;
Yet would be now, could I but have my wish,
Colder and dumber and deafer than a fish.   10

To a Wealthy Man Who Promised a Second
Subscription to the Dublin Municipal Gallery
if it Were Proved the People Wanted Pictures

You gave, but will not give again
Until enough of Paudeen's* pence
By Biddy's halfpennies have lain
To be "some sort of evidence",
Before you'll put your guineas down,
That things it were a pride to give
Are what the blind and ignorant town
Imagines best to make it thrive.
What cared Duke Ercole,* that bid
His mummers to the market-place,   10
What th' onion-sellers thought or did
So that his Plautus* set the pace
For the Italian comedies?
And Guidobaldo,* when he made
That grammar school of courtesies
Where wit and beauty learned their trade
Upon Urbino's windy hill,
Had sent no runners to and fro
That he might learn the shepherds' will.
And when they drove out Cosimo,*   20
Indifferent how the rancour ran,
He gave the hours they had set free
To Michelozzo's* latest plan
For the San Marco Library,
Whence turbulent Italy should draw
Delight in Art whose end is peace,
In logic and in natural law
By sucking at the dugs of Greece.

Your open hand but shows our loss,
For he knew better how to live.   30
Let Paudeens play at pitch and toss,

24

Look up in the sun's eye and give
What the exultant heart calls good
That some new day may breed the best
Because you gave, not what they would,
But the right twigs for an eagle's nest!

September 1913

What need you, being come to sense,
But fumble in a greasy till
And add the halfpence to the pence
And prayer to shivering prayer, until
You have dried the marrow from the bone;
For men were born to pray and save:
Romantic Ireland's dead and gone,
It's with O'Leary* in the grave.

Yet they were of a different kind,
The names that stilled your childish play,   10
They have gone about the world like wind,
But little time had they to pray
For whom the hangman's rope was spun,
And what, God help us, could they save?
Romantic Ireland's dead and gone,
It's with O'Leary in the grave.

Was it for this the wild geese* spread
The grey wing upon every tide;
For this that all that blood was shed,
For this Edward Fitzgerald* died,   20
And Robert Emmet* and Wolfe Tone,*
All that delirium of the brave?
Romantic Ireland's dead and gone,
It's with O'Leary in the grave.

Yet could we turn the years again,
And call those exiles as they were,
In all their loneliness and pain,
You'd cry, "Some woman's yellow hair
Has maddened every mother's son":
They weighed so lightly what they gave.   30
But let them be, they're dead and gone,
They're with O'Leary in the grave.

When Helen Lived

We have cried in our despair
That men desert,
For some trivial affair
Or noisy, insolent sport,
Beauty that we have won
From bitterest hours;
Yet we, had we walked within
Those topless towers
Where Helen walked with her boy,
Had given but as the rest   10
Of the men and women of Troy,
A word and a jest.

Fallen Majesty

Although crowds gathered once if she but showed her face,
And even old men's eyes grew dim, this hand alone,
Like some last courtier at a gypsy camping place
Babbling of fallen majesty, records what's gone.

The lineaments, a heart that laughter has made sweet,
These, these remain, but I record what's gone. A crowd
Will gather, and not know it walks the very street
Whereon a thing once walked that seemed a burning cloud.

Friends

Now must I these three praise –
Three women that have wrought
What joy is in my days:
One because no thought,
Nor those unpassing cares,
No, not in these fifteen
Many-times-troubled years,
Could ever come between
Mind and delighted mind;
And one because her hand   10
Had strength that could unbind
What none can understand,
What none can have and thrive,
Youth's dreamy load, till she
So changed me that I live
Labouring in ecstasy.
And what of her that took
All till my youth was gone
With scarce a pitying look?
How could I praise that one?   20
When day begins to break
I count my good and bad,
Being wakeful for her sake,
Remembering what she had,
What eagle look still shows,
While up from my heart's root
So great a sweetness flows
I shake from head to foot.

That the Night Come

She lived in storm and strife,
Her soul had such desire
For what proud death may bring
That it could not endure
The common good of life,
But lived as 'twere a king
That packed his marriage day
With banneret and pennon,
Trumpet and kettledrum,
And the outrageous cannon,   10
To bundle time away
That the night come.

A Coat

I made my song a coat
Covered with embroideries
Out of old mythologies
From heel to throat;
But the fools caught it,
Wore it in the world's eyes
As though they'd wrought it.
Song, let them take it
For there's more enterprise
In walking naked. 10

While I, from That Reed-throated Whisperer...

While I, from that reed-throated whisperer
Who comes at need, although not now as once
A clear articulation in the air,
But inwardly, surmise companions
Beyond the fling of the dull ass's hoof
– Ben Jonson's phrase – and find when June is come
At Kyle-na-no under that ancient roof
A sterner conscience and a friendlier home,
I can forgive even that wrong of wrongs,
Those undreamt accidents that have made me   10
– Seeing that Fame has perished this long while,
Being but a part of ancient ceremony –
Notorious, till all my priceless things
Are but a post the passing dogs defile.

*In Memory of Major Robert Gregory**

I

Now that we're almost settled in our house
I'll name the friends that cannot sup with us
Beside a fire of turf in th' ancient tower,
And having talked to some late hour
Climb up the narrow winding stair to bed:
Discoverers of forgotten truth
Or mere companions of my youth,
All, all are in my thoughts tonight being dead.

II

Always we'd have the new friend meet the old
And we are hurt if either friend seem cold,   10
And there is salt to lengthen out the smart
In the affections of our heart,
And quarrels are blown up upon that head,
But not a friend that I would bring
This night can set us quarrelling,
For all that come into my mind are dead.

III

Lionel Johnson* comes the first to mind,
That loved his learning better than mankind,
Though courteous to the worst; much falling he
Brooded upon sanctity   20
Till all his Greek and Latin learning seemed
A long blast upon the horn that brought
A little nearer to his thought
A measureless consummation that he dreamed.

IV

And that enquiring man John Synge* comes next,
That dying chose the living world for text

And never could have rested in the tomb
But that, long travelling, he had come
Towards nightfall upon certain set apart
In a most desolate stony place,   30
Towards nightfall upon a race
Passionate and simple like his heart.

                              V

And then I think of old George Pollexfen,*
In muscular youth well known to Mayo men
For horsemanship at meets or at racecourses,
That could have shown how pure-bred horses
And solid men, for all their passion, live
But as the outrageous stars incline
By opposition, square and trine,
Having grown sluggish and contemplative.   40

                              VI

They were my close companions many a year,
A portion of my mind and life, as it were,
And now their breathless faces seem to look
Out of some old picture book;
I am accustomed to their lack of breath,
But not that my dear friend's dear son,
Our Sidney* and our perfect man,
Could share in that discourtesy of death.

                              VII

For all things the delighted eye now sees
Were loved by him; the old storm-broken trees   50
That cast their shadows upon road and bridge;
The tower set on the stream's edge;
The ford where drinking cattle make a stir
Nightly, and startled by that sound
The water hen must change her ground;
He might have been your heartiest welcomer.

VIII

When with the Galway foxhounds he would ride
From Castle Taylor to the Roxborough side
Or Esserkelly plain, few kept his pace;
At Mooneen he had leaped a place   60
So perilous that half the astonished meet
Had shut their eyes, and where was it
He rode a race without a bit?
And yet his mind outran the horses' feet.

IX

We dreamed that a great painter had been born
To cold Clare rock and Galway rock and thorn,
To that stern colour and that delicate line
That are our secret discipline
Wherein the gazing heart doubles her might.
Soldier, scholar, horseman, he,   70
And yet he had the intensity
To have published all to be a world's delight.

X

What other could so well have counselled us
In all lovely intricacies of a house
As he that practised or that understood
All work in metal or in wood,
In moulded plaster or in carven stone?
Soldier, scholar, horseman, he,
And all he did done perfectly
As though he had but that one trade alone.   80

XI

Some burn damp faggots, others may consume
The entire combustible world in one small room
As though dried straw, and if we turn about
The bare chimney is gone black out
Because the work had finished in that flare.
Soldier, scholar, horseman, he,
As 'twere all life's epitome.
What made us dream that he could comb grey hair?

XII

I had thought, seeing how bitter is that wind
That shakes the shutter, to have brought to mind   90
All those that manhood tried, or childhood loved
Or boyish intellect approved,
With some appropriate commentary on each;
Until imagination brought
A fitter welcome, but a thought
Of that late death took all my heart for speech.

An Irish Airman Foresees His Death

I know that I shall meet my fate
Somewhere among the clouds above;
Those that I fight I do not hate,
Those that I guard I do not love;
My country is Kiltartan Cross,
My countrymen Kiltartan's poor,
No likely end could bring them loss
Or leave them happier than before.
Nor law, nor duty bade me fight,
Nor public men, nor cheering crowds,   10
A lonely impulse of delight
Drove to this tumult in the clouds;
I balanced all, brought all to mind,
The years to come seemed waste of breath,
A waste of breath the years behind
In balance with this life, this death.

To a Young Beauty

Dear fellow-artist, why so free
With every sort of company,
With every Jack and Jill?
Choose your companions from the best;
Who draws a bucket with the rest
Soon topples down the hill.

You may, that mirror for a school,
Be passionate, not bountiful
As common beauties may,
Who were not born to keep in trim   10
With old Ezekiel's cherubim*
But those of Beauvarlet.*

I know what wages beauty gives,
How hard a life her servant lives,
Yet praise the winters gone:
There is not a fool can call me friend,
And I may dine at journey's end
With Landor* and with Donne.

The Scholars

Bald heads forgetful of their sins,
Old, learned, respectable bald heads
Edit and annotate the lines
That young men, tossing on their beds,
Rhymed out in love's despair
To flatter beauty's ignorant ear.

All shuffle there; all cough in ink;
All wear the carpet with their shoes;
All think what other people think;
All know the man their neighbour knows.   10
Lord, what would they say
Did their Catullus* walk that way?

Her Praise

She is foremost of those that I would hear praised.
I have gone about the house, gone up and down
As a man does who has published a new book,
Or a young girl dressed out in her new gown,
And though I have turned the talk by hook or crook
Until her praise should be the uppermost theme,
A woman spoke of some new tale she had read,
A man confusedly in a half dream
As though some other name ran in his head.
She is foremost of those that I would hear praised.   10
I will talk no more of books or the long war
But walk by the dry thorn until I have found
Some beggar sheltering from the wind, and there
Manage the talk until her name come round.
If there be rags enough he will know her name
And be well pleased remembering it, for in the old days,
Though she had young men's praise and old men's blame,
Among the poor both old and young gave her praise.

Broken Dreams

There is grey in your hair.
Young men no longer suddenly catch their breath
When you are passing;
But maybe some old gaffer mutters a blessing
Because it was your prayer
Recovered him upon the bed of death.
For your sole sake – that all heart's ache have known,
And given to others all heart's ache,
From meagre girlhood's putting on
Burdensome beauty – for your sole sake   10
Heaven has put away the stroke of her doom,
So great her portion in that peace you make
By merely walking in a room.

Your beauty can but leave among us
Vague memories, nothing but memories.
A young man when the old men are done talking
Will say to an old man, "Tell me of that lady
The poet stubborn with his passion sang us
When age might well have chilled his blood."

Vague memories, nothing but memories,   20
But in the grave all, all, shall be renewed.
The certainty that I shall see that lady
Leaning or standing or walking
In the first loveliness of womanhood,
And with the fervour of my youthful eyes,
Has set me muttering like a fool.

You are more beautiful than anyone,
And yet your body had a flaw:
Your small hands were not beautiful,
And I am afraid that you will run   30
And paddle to the wrist

In that mysterious, always brimming lake
Where those that have obeyed the holy law
Paddle and are perfect. Leave unchanged
The hands that I have kissed,
For old sake's sake.

The last stroke of midnight dies.
All day in the one chair
From dream to dream and rhyme to rhyme I have ranged
In rambling talk with an image of air: 40
Vague memories, nothing but memories.

*Ego Dominus Tuus**

*Hic.** On the grey sand beside the shallow stream
Under your old wind-beaten tower, where still
A lamp burns on beside the open book
That Michael Robartes* left, you walk in the moon
And though you have passed the best of life still trace,
Enthralled by the unconquerable delusion,
Magical shapes.

*Ille.**   By the help of an image
I call to my own opposite, summon all
That I have handled least, least looked upon.

Hic. And I would find myself and not an image.   10

Ille. That is our modern hope, and by its light
We have lit upon the gentle, sensitive mind
And lost the old nonchalance of the hand;
Whether we have chosen chisel, pen or brush,
We are but critics, or but half create,
Timid, entangled, empty and abashed,
Lacking the countenance of our friends.

Hic.   And yet
The chief imagination of Christendom,
Dante Alighieri, so utterly found himself
That he has made that hollow face of his   20
More plain to the mind's eye than any face
But that of Christ.

Ille.   And did he find himself,
Or was the hunger that had made it hollow
A hunger for the apple on the bough
Most out of reach? And is that spectral image
The man that Lapo and that Guido* knew?

I think he fashioned from his opposite
An image that might have been a stony face
Staring upon a Bedouin's horse-hair roof
From doored and windowed cliff, or half upturned   30
Among the coarse grass and the camel-dung.
He set his chisel to the hardest stone.
Being mocked by Guido for his lecherous life,
Derided and deriding, driven out
To climb that stair and eat that bitter bread,
He found the unpersuadable justice, he found
The most exalted lady loved by a man.

Hic. Yet surely there are men who have made their art
Out of no tragic war, lovers of life,
Impulsive men that look for happiness   40
And sing when they have found it.

Ille.   No, not sing,
For those that love the world serve it in action,
Grow rich, popular and full of influence,
And should they paint or write, still it is action:
The struggle of the fly in marmalade.
The rhetorician would deceive his neighbours,
The sentimentalist himself; while art
Is but a vision of reality.
What portion in the world can the artist have
Who has awakened from the common dream   50
But dissipation and despair?

Hic.   And yet
No one denies to Keats love of the world;
Remember his deliberate happiness.

Ille. His art is happy, but who knows his mind?
I see a schoolboy when I think of him,
With face and nose pressed to a sweet-shop window,
For certainly he sank into his grave
His senses and his heart unsatisfied,

And made – being poor, ailing and ignorant,
Shut out from all the luxury of the world, 60
The coarse-bred son of a livery-stable keeper –
Luxuriant song.

Hic. Why should you leave the lamp
Burning alone beside an open book,
And trace these characters upon the sands?
A style is found by sedentary toil
And by the imitation of great masters.

Ille. Because I seek an image, not a book.
Those men that in their writings are most wise
Own nothing but their blind, stupefied hearts.
I call to the mysterious one who yet 70
Shall walk the wet sands by the edge of the stream
And look most like me, being indeed my double,
And prove of all imaginable things
The most unlike, being my anti-self,
And standing by these characters disclose
All that I seek, and whisper it as though
He were afraid the birds, who cry aloud
Their momentary cries before it is dawn,
Would carry it away to blasphemous men.

Easter, 1916

I have met them at close of day
Coming with vivid faces
From counter or desk among grey
Eighteenth-century houses.
I have passed with a nod of the head
Or polite meaningless words,
Or have lingered awhile and said
Polite meaningless words,
And thought before I had done
Of a mocking tale or a gibe   10
To please a companion
Around the fire at the club,
Being certain that they and I
But lived where motley is worn:
All changed, changed utterly:
A terrible beauty is born.

That woman's days were spent
In ignorant goodwill,
Her nights in argument
Until her voice grew shrill.   20
What voice more sweet than hers
When, young and beautiful,
She rode to harriers?
This man had kept a school
And rode our wingèd horse;
This other his helper and friend
Was coming into his force;
He might have won fame in the end,
So sensitive his nature seemed,
So daring and sweet his thought.   30
This other man I had dreamed
A drunken, vainglorious lout.
He had done most bitter wrong

To some who are near my heart,
Yet I number him in the song;
He, too, has resigned his part
In the casual comedy;
He, too, has been changed in his turn,
Transformed utterly:
A terrible beauty is born.   40

Hearts with one purpose alone
Through summer and winter seem
Enchanted to a stone
To trouble the living stream.
The horse that comes from the road,
The rider, the birds that range
From cloud to tumbling cloud,
Minute by minute they change;
A shadow of cloud on the stream
Changes minute by minute;   50
A horse hoof slides on the brim,
And a horse plashes within it;
The long-legged moor hens dive,
And hens to moor cocks call;
Minute by minute they live:
The stone's in the midst of all.

Too long a sacrifice
Can make a stone of the heart.
Oh when may it suffice?
That is Heaven's part, our part   60
To murmur name upon name,
As a mother names her child
When sleep at last has come
On limbs that had run wild.
What is it but nightfall?
No, no, not night but death;
Was it needless death after all?
For England may keep faith
For all that is done and said.

We know their dream – enough   70
To know they dreamed and are dead,
And what if excess of love
Bewildered them till they died?
I write it out in a verse –
MacDonagh and MacBride
And Connolly and Pearse*
Now and in time to be,
Wherever green is worn,
Are changed, changed utterly:
A terrible beauty is born.   80

Sixteen Dead Men

O but we talked at large before
The sixteen men were shot,
But who can talk of give and take,
What should be and what not
While those dead men are loitering there
To stir the boiling pot?

You say that we should still the land
Till Germany's overcome;
But who is there to argue that
Now Pearse* is deaf and dumb?   10
And is their logic to outweigh
MacDonagh's* bony thumb?

How could you dream they'd listen
That have an ear alone
For those new comrades they have found,
Lord Edward and Wolfe Tone,*
Or meddle with our give and take
That converse bone to bone?

The Rose Tree

"Oh words are lightly spoken,"
Said Pearse to Connolly,*
"Maybe a breath of politic words
Has withered our Rose Tree,
Or maybe but a wind that blows
Across the bitter sea."

"It needs to be but watered,"
James Connolly replied,
"To make the green come out again
And spread on every side,   10
And shake the blossom from the bud
To be the garden's pride."

"But where can we draw water,"
Said Pearse to Connolly,
"When all the wells are parched away?
Oh plain as plain can be
There's nothing but our own red blood
Can make a right Rose Tree."

On a Political Prisoner

She that but little patience knew,
From childhood on, had now so much
A grey gull lost its fear and flew
Down to her cell and there alit,
And there endured her fingers' touch
And from her fingers ate its bit.

Did she in touching that lone wing
Recall the years before her mind
Became a bitter, an abstract thing,
Her thought some popular enmity: 10
Blind and leader of the blind
Drinking the foul ditch where they lie?

When long ago I saw her ride
Under Ben Bulben to the meet,
The beauty of her countryside
With all youth's lonely wildness stirred,
She seemed to have grown clean and sweet
Like any rock-bred, sea-borne bird:

Sea-borne, or balanced on the air
When first it sprang out of the nest   20
Upon some lofty rock to stare
Upon the cloudy canopy,
While under its storm-beaten breast
Cried out the hollows of the sea.

The Second Coming

Turning and turning in the widening gyre
The falcon cannot hear the falconer;
Things fall apart; the centre cannot hold;
Mere anarchy is loosed upon the world,
The blood-dimmed tide is loosed, and everywhere
The ceremony of innocence is drowned;
The best lack all conviction, while the worst
Are full of passionate intensity.

Surely some revelation is at hand;
Surely the Second Coming is at hand.   10
The Second Coming! Hardly are those words out
When a vast image out of *Spiritus Mundi**
Troubles my sight: somewhere in the sands of the desert
A shape with lion body and the head of a man,
A gaze blank and pitiless as the sun,
Is moving its slow thighs, while all about it
Reel shadows of the indignant desert birds.
The darkness drops again, but now I know
That twenty centuries of stony sleep
Were vexed to nightmare by a rocking cradle,   20
And what rough beast, its hour come round at last,
Slouches towards Bethlehem to be born?

A Prayer for my Daughter

Once more the storm is howling, and half hid
Under this cradle hood and coverlid
My child sleeps on. There is no obstacle
But Gregory's wood and one bare hill
Whereby the haystack- and roof-levelling wind,
Bred on the Atlantic, can be stayed;
And for an hour I have walked and prayed
Because of the great gloom that is in my mind.

I have walked and prayed for this young child an hour
And heard the sea wind scream upon the tower,   10
And under the arches of the bridge, and scream
In the elms above the flooded stream;
Imagining in excited reverie
That the future years had come,
Dancing to a frenzied drum,
Out of the murderous innocence of the sea.

May she be granted beauty and yet not
Beauty to make a stranger's eye distraught,
Or hers before a looking glass, for such,
Being made beautiful overmuch,   20
Consider beauty a sufficient end,
Lose natural kindness and maybe
The heart-revealing intimacy
That chooses right, and never find a friend.

Helen, being chosen, found life flat and dull
And later had much trouble from a fool,
While that great Queen,* that rose out of the spray,
Being fatherless could have her way
Yet chose a bandy-leggèd smith* for man.
It's certain that fine women eat   30

53

A crazy salad with their meat
Whereby the Horn of Plenty is undone.

In courtesy I'd have her chiefly learned;
Hearts are not had as a gift but hearts are earned
By those that are not entirely beautiful;
Yet many, that have played the fool
For beauty's very self, has charm made wise,
And many a poor man that has roved,
Loved and thought himself beloved,
From a glad kindness cannot take his eyes.   40

May she become a flourishing hidden tree
That all her thoughts may like the linnet be,
And have no business but dispensing round
Their magnanimities of sound,
Nor but in merriment begin a chase,
Nor but in merriment a quarrel.
O may she live like some green laurel
Rooted in one dear perpetual place.

My mind, because the minds that I have loved,
The sort of beauty that I have approved,   50
Prosper but little, has dried up of late,
Yet knows that to be choked with hate
May well be of all evil chances chief.
If there's no hatred in a mind
Assault and battery of the wind
Can never tear the linnet from the leaf.

An intellectual hatred is the worst,
So let her think opinions are accursed.
Have I not seen the loveliest woman born
Out of the mouth of Plenty's horn,   60
Because of her opinionated mind
Barter that horn and every good
By quiet natures understood
For an old bellows full of angry wind?

Considering that, all hatred driven hence,
The soul recovers radical innocence
And learns at last that it is self-delighting,
Self-appeasing, self-affrighting,
And that its own sweet will is Heaven's will;
She can, though every face should scowl   70
And every windy quarter howl
Or every bellows burst, be happy still.

And may her bridegroom bring her to a house
Where all's accustomed, ceremonious;
For arrogance and hatred are the wares
Peddled in the thoroughfares.
How but in custom and in ceremony
Are innocence and beauty born?
Ceremony's a name for the rich horn,
And custom for the spreading laurel tree.   80

Sailing to Byzantium

I

That is no country for old men. The young
In one another's arms, birds in the trees –
Those dying generations – at their song,
The salmon-falls, the mackerel-crowded seas,
Fish, flesh, or fowl, commend all summer long
Whatever is begotten, born, and dies.
Caught in that sensual music all neglect
Monuments of unageing intellect.

II

An aged man is but a paltry thing,
A tattered coat upon a stick, unless   10
Soul clap its hands and sing, and louder sing
For every tatter in its mortal dress,
Nor is there singing school but studying
Monuments of its own magnificence;
And therefore I have sailed the seas and come
To the holy city of Byzantium.

III

O sages standing in God's holy fire
As in the gold mosaic of a wall,
Come from the holy fire, perne in a gyre,
And be the singing masters of my soul.   20
Consume my heart away – sick with desire
And fastened to a dying animal,
It knows not what it is – and gather me
Into the artifice of eternity.

IV

Once out of nature I shall never take
My bodily form from any natural thing,
But such a form as Grecian goldsmiths make

Of hammered gold and gold enamelling
To keep a drowsy Emperor awake;
Or set upon a golden bough to sing   30
To lords and ladies of Byzantium
Of what is past, or passing, or to come.

The Tower

I

What shall I do with this absurdity –
O heart, O troubled heart – this caricature,
Decrepit age that has been tied to me
As to a dog's tail?
                              Never had I more
Excited, passionate, fantastical
Imagination, nor an ear and eye
That more expected the impossible –
No, not in boyhood when with rod and fly,
Or the humbler worm, I climbed Ben Bulben's back
And had the livelong summer day to spend.   10
It seems that I must bid the Muse go pack,
Choose Plato and Plotinus* for a friend
Until imagination, ear and eye,
Can be content with argument and deal
In abstract things, or be derided by
A sort of battered kettle at the heel.

II

I pace upon the battlements and stare
On the foundations of a house, or where
Tree, like a sooty finger, starts from the earth,
And send imagination forth   20
Under the day's declining beam, and call
Images and memories
From ruin or from ancient trees,
For I would ask a question of them all.

Beyond that ridge lived Mrs French,* and once
When every silver candlestick or sconce
Lit up the dark mahogany and the wine,
A serving man, that could divine
That most respected lady's every wish,

Ran and with the garden shears 30
Clipped an insolent farmer's ears
And brought them in a little covered dish.

Some few remembered still when I was young
A peasant girl commended by a song,
Who'd lived somewhere upon that rocky place,
And praised the colour of her face,
And had the greater joy in praising her,
Remembering that, if walked she there,
Farmers jostled at the fair
So great a glory did the song confer. 40

And certain men, being maddened by those rhymes,
Or else by toasting her a score of times,
Rose from the table and declared it right
To test their fancy by their sight,
But they mistook the brightness of the moon
For the prosaic light of day –
Music had driven their wits astray –
And one was drowned in the great bog of Cloone.

Strange, but the man who made the song was blind;
Yet, now I have considered it, I find 50
That nothing strange; the tragedy began
With Homer that was a blind man,
And Helen has all living hearts betrayed.
Oh may the moon and sunlight seem
One inextricable beam,
For if I triumph I must make men mad.

And I myself created Hanrahan*
And drove him drunk or sober through the dawn
From somewhere in the neighbouring cottages:
Caught by an old man's juggleries 50
He stumbled, tumbled, fumbled to and fro
And had but broken knees for hire

And horrible splendour of desire;
I thought it all out twenty years ago:

Good fellows shuffled cards in an old bawn,
And when that ancient ruffian's turn was on
He so bewitched the cards under his thumb
That all but the one card became
A pack of hounds and not a pack of cards,
And that he changed into a hare.   60
Hanrahan rose in frenzy there
And followed up those baying creatures towards –

Oh towards I have forgotten what – enough!
I must recall a man that neither love
Nor music nor an enemy's clipped ear
Could, he was so harried, cheer;
A figure that has grown so fabulous
There's not a neighbour left to say
When he finished his dog's day:
An ancient bankrupt master of this house.   70

Before that ruin came, for centuries,
Rough men-at-arms, cross-gartered to the knees
Or shod in iron, climbed the narrow stairs,
And certain men-at-arms there were
Whose images, in the Great Memory stored,
Come with loud cry and panting breast
To break upon a sleeper's rest
While their great wooden dice beat on the board.

As I would question all, come all who can;
Come old, necessitous, half-mounted man;   80
And bring beauty's blind rambling celebrant;
The red man the juggler sent
Through godforsaken meadows; Mrs French,
Gifted with so fine an ear;
The man drowned in a bog's mire,
When mocking Muses chose the country wench.

Did all old men and women, rich and poor,
Who trod upon these rocks or passed this door,
Whether in public or in secret rage
As I do now against old age? 90
But I have found an answer in those eyes
That are impatient to be gone;
Go therefore, but leave Hanrahan,
For I need all his mighty memories.

Old lecher with a love on every wind,
Bring up out of that deep considering mind
All that you have discovered in the grave,
For it is certain that you have
Reckoned up every unforeknown, unseeing
Plunge, lured by a softening eye, 100
Or by a touch or a sigh,
Into the labyrinth of another's being;

Does the imagination dwell the most
Upon a woman won or woman lost?
If on the lost, admit you turned aside
From a great labyrinth out of pride,
Cowardice, some silly over-subtle thought
Or anything called conscience once,
And that if memory recur, the sun's
Under eclipse and the day blotted out. 110

III

It is time that I wrote my will;
I choose upstanding men
That climb the streams until
The fountain leap, and at dawn
Drop their cast at the side
Of dripping stone; I declare
They shall inherit my pride,
The pride of people that were
Bound neither to Cause nor to State.
Neither to slaves that were spat on, 120

Nor to the tyrants that spat,
The people of Burke and of Grattan*
That gave, though free to refuse –
Pride, like that of the morn,
When the headlong light is loose,
Or that of the fabulous horn,
Or that of the sudden shower
When all streams are dry,
Or that of the hour
When the swan must fix his eye   130
Upon a fading gleam,
Float out upon a long
Last reach of glittering stream
And there sing his last song.
And I declare my faith:
I mock Plotinus' thought
And cry in Plato's teeth,
Death and life were not
Till man made up the whole,
Made lock, stock and barrel   140
Out of his bitter soul,
Ay, sun and moon and star, all,
And further add to that
That, being dead, we rise,
Dream and so create
Translunar Paradise.
I have prepared my peace
With learned Italian things
And the proud stones of Greece,
Poet's imaginings   150
And memories of love,
Memories of the words of women,
All those things whereof
Man makes a superhuman
Mirror-resembling dream.

As at the loophole there
The daws chatter and scream,

And drop twigs layer upon layer.
When they have mounted up,
The mother bird will rest   160
On their hollow top,
And so warm her wild nest.

I leave both faith and pride
To young upstanding men
Climbing the mountain side,
That under bursting dawn
They may drop a fly,
Being of that metal made
Till it was broken by
This sedentary trade.   170

Now shall I make my soul,
Compelling it to study
In a learned school
Till the wreck of body,
Slow decay of blood,
Testy delirium
Or dull decrepitude,
Or what worse evil come –
The death of friends, or death
Of every brilliant eye   180
That made a catch in the breath –
Seem but the clouds of the sky
When the horizon fades,
Or a bird's sleepy cry
Among the deepening shades.

Meditations in Time of Civil War

I

Ancestral Houses

Surely among a rich man's flowering lawns,
Amid the rustle of his planted hills,
Life overflows without ambitious pains;
And rains down life until the basin spills,
And mounts more dizzy high the more it rains
As though to choose whatever shape it wills
And never stoop to a mechanical
Or servile shape, at others' beck and call.

Mere dreams, mere dreams! Yet Homer had not sung
Had he not found it certain beyond dreams   10
That out of life's own self-delight had sprung
The abounding glittering jet; though now it seems
As if some marvellous empty seashell flung
Out of the obscure dark of the rich streams,
And not a fountain, were the symbol which
Shadows the inherited glory of the rich.

Some violent bitter man, some powerful man
Called architect and artist in, that they,
Bitter and violent men, might rear in stone
The sweetness that all longed for night and day,   20
The gentleness none there had ever known;
But when the master's buried mice can play,
And maybe the great-grandson of that house,
For all its bronze and marble, 's but a mouse.

Oh what if gardens where the peacock strays
With delicate feet upon old terraces,
Or else all Juno from an urn displays
Before the indifferent garden deities;

Oh what if levelled lawns and gravelled ways
Where slippered Contemplation finds his ease   30
And Childhood a delight for every sense,
But take our greatness with our violence?

What if the glory of escutcheoned doors,
And buildings that a haughtier age designed,
The pacing to and fro on polished floors
Amid great chambers and long galleries, lined
With famous portraits of our ancestors;
What if those things the greatest of mankind
Consider most to magnify, or to bless,
But take our greatness with our bitterness?   40

II
My House

An ancient bridge, and a more ancient tower,
A farmhouse that is sheltered by its wall,
An acre of stony ground,
Where the symbolic rose can break in flower,
Old ragged elms, old thorns innumerable,
The sound of the rain or sound
Of every wind that blows;
The stilted water hen
Crossing stream again
Scared by the splashing of a dozen cows;   10

A winding stair, a chamber arched with stone,
A grey stone fireplace with an open hearth,
A candle and written page.
Il Penseroso's Platonist* toiled on
In some like chamber, shadowing forth
How the demonic rage
Imagined everything.
Benighted travellers
From markets and from fairs
Have seen his midnight candle glimmering.   20

Two men have founded here. A man-at-arms
Gathered a score of horse and spent his days
In this tumultuous spot,
Where through long wars and sudden night alarms
His dwindling score and he seemed castaways
Forgetting and forgot;
And I, that after me
My bodily heirs may find,
To exalt a lonely mind,
Befitting emblems of adversity.   30

III
My Table

Two heavy trestles, and a board
Where Sato's gift, a changeless sword,*
By pen and paper lies,
That it may moralize
My days out of their aimlessness.
A bit of an embroidered dress
Covers its wooden sheath.
Chaucer had not drawn breath
When it was forged. In Sato's house,
Curved like new moon, moon-luminous,   10
It lay five hundred years.
Yet if no change appears
No moon; only an aching heart
Conceives a changeless work of art.
Our learned men have urged
That when and where 'twas forged
A marvellous accomplishment,
In painting or in pottery, went
From father unto son
And through the centuries ran   20
And seemed unchanging like the sword.
Soul's beauty being most adored,
Men and their business took
The soul's unchanging look;

For the most rich inheritor,
Knowing that none could pass heaven's door
That loved inferior art,
Had such an aching heart
That he, although a country's talk
For silken clothes and stately walk,   30
Had waking wits; it seemed
Juno's peacock screamed.

IV
My Descendants

Having inherited a vigorous mind
From my old fathers, I must nourish dreams
And leave a woman and a man behind
As vigorous of mind, and yet it seems
Life scarce can cast a fragrance on the wind,
Scarce spread a glory to the morning beams,
But the torn petals strew the garden plot,
And there's but common greenness after that.

And what if my descendants lose the flower
Through natural declension of the soul,   10
Through too much business with the passing hour,
Through too much play, or marriage with a fool?
May this laborious stair and this stark tower
Become a roofless ruin that the owl
May build in the cracked masonry and cry
Her desolation to the desolate sky.

The Primum Mobile that fashioned us
Has made the very owls in circles move;
And I, that count myself most prosperous,
Seeing that love and friendship are enough,   20
For an old neighbour's friendship chose the house
And decked and altered it for a girl's love,
And know whatever flourish and decline
These stones remain their monument and mine.

V

The Road at My Door

An affable Irregular,*
A heavily built Falstaffian man,
Comes cracking jokes of civil war
As though to die by gunshot were
The finest play under the sun.

A brown Lieutenant* and his men,
Half dressed in national uniform,
Stand at my door, and I complain
Of the foul weather, hail and rain,
A pear tree broken by the storm.   10

I count those feathered balls of soot
The moor hen guides upon the stream,
To silence the envy in my thought,
And turn towards my chamber, caught
In the cold snows of a dream.

VI

The Stare's Nest by My Window

The bees build in the crevices
Of loosening masonry, and there
The mother birds bring grubs and flies.
My wall is loosening; honey bees,
Come build in the empty house of the stare.

We are closed in, and the key is turned
On our uncertainty; somewhere
A man is killed, or a house burned,
Yet no clear fact to be discerned:
Come build in the empty house of the stare.   10

A barricade of stone or of wood;
Some fourteen days of civil war;

Last night they trundled down the road
That dead young soldier in his blood:
Come build in the empty house of the stare.

We had fed the heart on fantasies,
The heart's grown brutal from the fare;
More substance in our enmities
Than in our love; O honey bees,
Come build in the empty house of the stare.   20

VII
I See Phantoms of Hatred and of the Heart's Fullness and of the Coming Emptiness

I climb to the tower top and lean upon broken stone,
A mist that is like blown snow is sweeping over all,
Valley, river and elms, under the light of a moon
That seems unlike itself, that seems unchangeable,
A glittering sword out of the east. A puff of wind
And those white glimmering fragments of the mist sweep by.
Frenzies bewilder, reveries perturb the mind;
Monstrous familiar images swim to the mind's eye.

"Vengeance upon the murderers," the cry goes up,
"Vengeance for Jacques Molay."* In cloud-pale rags, or in lace,   10
The rage-driven, rage-tormented and rage-hungry troop,
Trooper belabouring trooper, biting at arm or at face,
Plunges towards nothing, arms and fingers spreading wide
For the embrace of nothing, and I, my wits astray
Because of all that senseless tumult, all but cried
For vengeance on the murderers of Jacques Molay.

Their legs long, delicate and slender, aquamarine their eyes,
Magical unicorns bear ladies on their backs.
The ladies close their musing eyes. No prophecies,
Remembered out of Babylonian almanacs,   20
Have closed the ladies' eyes, their minds are but a pool
Where even longing drowns under its own excess;

Nothing but stillness can remain when hearts are full
Of their own sweetness, bodies of their loveliness.

The cloud-pale unicorns, the eyes of aquamarine,
The quivering half-closed eyelids, the rags of cloud or of lace,
Or eyes that rage has brightened, arms it has made lean,
Give place to an indifferent multitude, give place
To brazen hawks. Nor self-delighting reverie,
Nor hate of what's to come, nor pity for what's gone,   30
Nothing but grip of claw, and the eye's complacency,
The innumerable clanging wings that have put out the moon.

I turn away and shut the door, and on the stair
Wonder how many times I could have proved my worth
In something that all others understand or share;
But O! ambitious heart, had such a proof drawn forth
A company of friends, a conscience set at ease,
It had but made us pine the more. The abstract joy,
The half-read wisdom of demonic images,
Suffice the ageing man as once the growing boy.   40

Nineteen Hundred and Nineteen

I

Many ingenious lovely things are gone
That seemed sheer miracle to the multitude,
Protected from the circle of the moon
That pitches common things about. There stood
Amid the ornamental bronze and stone
An ancient image made of olive wood –
And gone are Phidias' famous ivories
And all the golden grasshoppers and bees.

We too had many pretty toys when young;
A law indifferent to blame or praise,   10
To bribe or threat; habits that made old wrong
Melt down, as it were wax in the sun's rays;
Public opinion ripening for so long
We thought it would outlive all future days.
Oh what fine thought we had because we thought
That the worst rogues and rascals had died out.

All teeth were drawn, all ancient tricks unlearned,
And a great army but a showy thing;
What matter that no cannon had been turned
Into a ploughshare? Parliament and king   20
Thought that unless a little powder burned
The trumpeters might burst with trumpeting
And yet it lack all glory, and perchance
The guardsmen's drowsy chargers would not prance.

Now days are dragon-ridden, the nightmare
Rides upon sleep: a drunken soldiery
Can leave the mother, murdered at her door,
To crawl in her own blood, and go scot-free;
The night can sweat with terror as before
We pieced our thoughts into philosophy,   30

71

And planned to bring the world under a rule,
Who are but weasels fighting in a hole.

He who can read the signs nor sink unmanned
Into the half-deceit of some intoxicant
From shallow wits; who knows no work can stand,
Whether health, wealth or peace of mind were spent
On master-work of intellect or hand,
No honour leave its mighty monument,
Has but one comfort left: all triumph would
But break upon his ghostly solitude.   40

But is there any comfort to be found?
Man is in love and loves what vanishes,
What more is there to say? That country round
None dared admit, if such a thought were his,
Incendiary or bigot could be found
To burn that stump on the Acropolis,
Or break in bits the famous ivories
Or traffic in the grasshoppers or bees.

II
When Loie Fuller's Chinese dancers enwound
A shining web, a floating ribbon of cloth,   50
It seemed that a dragon of air
Had fallen among dancers, had whirled them round
Or hurried them off on its own furious path;
So the Platonic Year
Whirls out new right and wrong,
Whirls in the old instead;
All men are dancers and their tread
Goes to the barbarous clangour of a gong.

III
Some moralist or mythological poet
Compares the solitary soul to a swan;   60
I am satisfied with that,
Satisfied if a troubled mirror show it,
Before that brief gleam of its life be gone,

An image of its state;
The wings half spread for flight,
The breast thrust out in pride
Whether to play, or to ride
Those winds that clamour of approaching night.

A man in his own secret meditation
Is lost amid the labyrinth that he has made   70
In art or politics;
Some Platonist affirms that in the station
Where we should cast off body and trade
The ancient habit sticks,
And that if our works could
But vanish with our breath
That were a lucky death,
For triumph can but mar our solitude.

The swan has leaped into the desolate heaven:
That image can bring wildness, bring a rage   80
To end all things, to end
What my laborious life imagined, even
The half-imagined, the half-written page;
Oh but we dreamed to mend
Whatever mischief seemed
To afflict mankind, but now
That winds of winter blow
Learn that we were crack-pated when we dreamed.

IV
We, who seven years ago
Talked of honour and of truth,   90
Shriek with pleasure if we show
The weasel's twist, the weasel's tooth.

V
Come let us mock at the great
That had such burdens on the mind
And toiled so hard and late

To leave some monument behind,
Nor thought of the levelling wind.

Come let us mock at the wise;
With all those calendars whereon
They fixed old aching eyes,   100
They never saw how seasons run,
And now but gape at the sun.

Come let us mock at the good
That fancied goodness might be gay,
And sick of solitude
Might proclaim a holiday:
Wind shrieked – and where are they?

Mock mockers after that
That would not lift a hand maybe
To help good, wise or great   110
To bar that foul storm out, for we
Traffic in mockery.

VI

Violence upon the roads: violence of horses;
Some few have handsome riders, are garlanded
On delicate sensitive ear or tossing mane,
But wearied running round and round in their courses
All break and vanish, and evil gathers head:
Herodias'* daughters have returned again,
A sudden blast of dusty wind and after
Thunder of feet, tumult of images,   120
Their purpose in the labyrinth of the wind;
And should some crazy hand dare touch a daughter
All turn with amorous cries, or angry cries,
According to the wind, for all are blind.
But now wind drops, dust settles; thereupon
There lurches past, his great eyes without thought
Under the shadow of stupid straw-pale locks,
That insolent fiend Robert Artisson*
To whom the lovelorn Lady Kyteler* brought
Bronzed peacock feathers, red combs of her cocks.   130

Two Songs from a Play

I

I saw a staring virgin stand
Where holy Dionysus died,
And tear the heart out of his side,
And lay the heart upon her hand
And bear that beating heart away;
And then did all the Muses sing
Of Magnus Annus* at the spring,
As though God's death were but a play.

Another Troy must rise and set,
Another lineage feed the crow,   10
Another Argo's painted prow
Drive to a flashier bauble yet.
The Roman Empire stood appalled:
It dropped the reins of peace and war
When that fierce virgin and her Star
Out of the fabulous darkness called.

II

In pity for man's darkening thought
He walked that room and issued thence
In Galilean turbulence;
The Babylonian starlight brought   20
A fabulous, formless darkness in;
Odour of blood when Christ was slain
Made all Platonic tolerance vain
And vain all Doric discipline.

Everything that man esteems
Endures a moment or a day.
Love's pleasure drives his love away,
The painter's brush consumes his dreams;

The herald's cry, the soldier's tread
Exhaust his glory and his might: 30
Whatever flames upon the night
Man's own resinous heart has fed.

Leda and the Swan

A sudden blow: the great wings beating still
Above the staggering girl, her thighs caressed
By the dark webs, her nape caught in his bill,
He holds her helpless breast upon his breast.

How can those terrified vague fingers push
The feathered glory from her loosening thighs?
And how can body, laid in that white rush,
But feel the strange heart beating where it lies?

A shudder in the loins engenders there
The broken wall, the burning roof and tower   10
And Agamemnon dead.
                              Being so caught up,
So mastered by the brute blood of the air,
Did she put on his knowledge with his power
Before the indifferent beak could let her drop?

Among School Children

I

I walk through the long schoolroom questioning;
A kind old nun in a white hood replies;
The children learn to cipher and to sing,
To study reading books and history,
To cut and sew, be neat in everything
In the best modern way – the children's eyes
In momentary wonder stare upon
A sixty-year-old smiling public man.

II

I dream of a Ledaean body, bent
Above a sinking fire, a tale that she   10
Told of a harsh reproof, or trivial event
That changed some childish day to tragedy –
Told, and it seemed that our two natures blent
Into a sphere from youthful sympathy,
Or else, to alter Plato's parable,
Into the yolk and white of the one shell.

III

And thinking of that fit of grief or rage
I look upon one child or t'other there
And wonder if she stood so at that age –
For even daughters of the swan can share   20
Something of every paddler's heritage –
And had that colour upon cheek or hair,
And thereupon my heart is driven wild:
She stands before me as a living child.

IV

Her present image floats into the mind –
Did Quattrocento finger fashion it
Hollow of cheek as though it drank the wind

And took a mess of shadows for its meat?
And I, though never of Ledaean kind,
Had pretty plumage once – enough of that,   30
Better to smile on all that smile, and show
There is a comfortable kind of old scarecrow.

                            V
What youthful mother, a shape upon her lap
Honey of generation had betrayed,
And that must sleep, shriek, struggle to escape
As recollection or the drug decide,
Would think her son, did she but see that shape
With sixty or more winters on its head,
A compensation for the pang of his birth,
Or the uncertainty of his setting forth?   40

                           VI
Plato thought nature but a spume that plays
Upon a ghostly paradigm of things;
Solider Aristotle played the taws
Upon the bottom of a king of kings;
World-famous golden-thighed Pythagoras
Fingered upon a fiddlestick or strings
What a star sang and careless Muses heard:
Old clothes upon old sticks to scare a bird.

                           VII
Both nuns and mothers worship images,
But those the candles light are not as those   50
That animate a mother's reveries,
But keep a marble or a bronze repose.
And yet they too break hearts – O Presences
That passion, piety or affection knows,
And that all heavenly glory symbolize –
O self-born mockers of man's enterprise;

                          VIII
Labour is blossoming or dancing where
The body is not bruised to pleasure soul,

Nor beauty born out of its own despair,
Nor blear-eyed wisdom out of midnight oil.   60
O chestnut tree, great-rooted blossomer,
Are you the leaf, the blossom or the bole?
O body swayed to music, O brightening glance,
How can we know the dancer from the dance?

All Souls' Night

Epilogue to 'A Vision'

Midnight has come and the great Christ Church bell
And many a lesser bell sound through the room;
And it is All Souls' Night.
And two long glasses brimmed with muscatel
Bubble upon the table. A ghost may come;
For it is a ghost's right,
His element is so fine,
Being sharpened by his death,
To drink from the wine breath
While our gross palates drink from the whole wine.   10

I need some mind that, if the cannon sound
From every quarter of the world, can stay
Wound in mind's pondering,
As mummies in the mummy cloth are wound;
Because I have a marvellous thing to say,
A certain marvellous thing
None but the living mock,
Though not for sober ear;
It may be all that hear
Should laugh and weep an hour upon the clock.   20

Horton's* the first I call. He loved strange thought
And knew that sweet extremity of pride
That's called platonic love,
And that to such a pitch of passion wrought
Nothing could bring him, when his lady died,
Anodyne for his love.
Words were but wasted breath;
One dear hope had he:
The inclemency
Of that or the next winter would be death.   30

Two thoughts were so mixed up I could not tell
Whether of her or God he thought the most,
But think that his mind's eye,
When upward turned, on one sole image fell;
And that a slight companionable ghost,
Wild with divinity,
Had so lit up the whole
Immense miraculous house
The Bible promised us,
It seemed a goldfish swimming in a bowl.   40

On Florence Emery* I call the next,
Who, finding the first wrinkles on a face
Admired and beautiful,
And by foreknowledge of the future vexed –
Diminished beauty, multiplied commonplace –
Preferred to teach a school
Away from neighbour or friend,
Among dark skins, and there
Permit foul years to wear
Hidden from eyesight to the unnoticed end.   50

Before that end much had she ravelled out
From a discourse in figurative speech
By some learned Indian
On the soul's journey. How it is whirled about
Wherever the orbit of the moon can reach,
Until it plunge into the sun,
And there, free and yet fast,
Being both Chance and Choice,
Forget its broken toys
And sink into its own delight at last.   60

I call MacGregor Mathers* from his grave,
For in my first hard springtime we were friends,
Although of late estranged.
I thought him half a lunatic, half knave,
And told him so, but friendship never ends,

82

And what if mind seem changed,
And it seem changed with the mind,
When thoughts rise up unbid
On generous things that he did
And I grow half contented to be blind!   70

He had much industry at setting out,
Much boisterous courage, before loneliness
Had driven him crazed;
For meditations upon unknown thought
Make human intercourse grow less and less;
They are neither paid nor praised.
But he'd object to the host,
The glass because my glass;
A ghost-lover he was
And may have grown more arrogant being a ghost.   80

But names are nothing. What matter who it be,
So that his elements have grown so fine
The fume of muscatel
Can give his sharpened palate ecstasy
No living man can drink from the whole wine.
I have mummy truths to tell
Whereat the living mock,
Though not for sober ear,
For maybe all that hear
Should laugh and weep an hour upon the clock.   90

Such thought – such thought have I that hold it tight
Till meditation master all its parts,
Nothing can stay my glance
Until that glance run in the world's despite
To where the damned have howled away their hearts,
And where the blessed dance;
Such thought, that in it bound
I need no other thing,
Wound in mind's wandering
As mummies in the mummy cloth are wound.   100

*In Memory of Eva Gore-Booth and Con Markiewicz**

The light of evening, Lissadell,*
Great windows open to the south,
Two girls in silk kimonos, both
Beautiful, one a gazelle.
But a raving autumn shears
Blossom from the summer's wreath;
The older is condemned to death,
Pardoned, drags out lonely years
Conspiring among the ignorant.
I know not what the younger dreams –   10
Some vague Utopia – and she seems,
When withered old and skeleton-gaunt,
An image of such politics.
Many a time I think to seek
One or the other out and speak
Of that old Georgian mansion, mix
Pictures of the mind, recall
That table and the talk of youth,
Two girls in silk kimonos, both
Beautiful, one a gazelle.   20

Dear shadows, now you know it all,
All the folly of a fight
With a common wrong or right.
The innocent and the beautiful
Have no enemy but time;
Arise and bid me strike a match
And strike another till time catch;
Should the conflagration climb,
Run till all the sages know.
We the great gazebo built,   30
They convicted us of guilt;
Bid me strike a match and blow.

A Dialogue of Self and Soul

I

My Soul. I summon to the winding ancient stair;
Set all your mind upon the steep ascent,
Upon the broken, crumbling battlement,
Upon the breathless starlit air,
Upon the star that marks the hidden pole;
Fix every wandering thought upon
That quarter where all thought is done:
Who can distinguish darkness from the soul?

My Self. The consecrated blade upon my knees
Is Sato's ancient blade,* still as it was,   10
Still razor-keen, still like a looking glass
Unspotted by the centuries;
That flowering, silken, old embroidery, torn
From some court lady's dress and round
The wooden scabbard bound and wound,
Can, tattered, still protect, faded adorn.

My Soul. Why should the imagination of a man
Long past his prime remember things that are
Emblematical of love and war?
Think of ancestral night that can,   20
If but imagination scorn the earth
And intellect is wandering
To this and that and t'other thing,
Deliver from the crime of death and birth.

My Self. Montashigi, third of his family, fashioned it
Five hundred years ago, about it lie
Flowers from I know not what embroidery –
Heart's purple – and all these I set
For emblems of the day against the tower
Emblematical of the night,   30

And claim as by a soldier's right
A charter to commit the crime once more.

My Soul. Such fullness in that quarter overflows
And falls into the basin of the mind
That man is stricken deaf and dumb and blind,
For intellect no longer knows
Is from the *Ought*, or *Knower* from the *Known* –
That is to say, ascends to Heaven;
Only the dead can be forgiven,
But when I think of that my tongue's a stone.   40

II

My Self. A living man is blind and drinks his drop.
What matter if the ditches are impure?
What matter if I live it all once more?
Endure that toil of growing up;
The ignominy of boyhood; the distress
Of boyhood changing into man;
The unfinished man and his pain
Brought face to face with his own clumsiness;

The finished man among his enemies? –
How in the name of Heaven can he escape   50
That defiling and disfigured shape
The mirror of malicious eyes
Casts upon his eyes until at last
He thinks that shape must be his shape?
And what's the good of an escape
If honour find him in the wintry blast?

I am content to live it all again
And yet again, if it be life to pitch
Into the frog spawn of a blind man's ditch,
A blind man battering blind men;   60
Or into that most fecund ditch of all,
The folly that man does
Or must suffer, if he woos

A proud woman not kindred of his soul.
I am content to follow to its source
Every event in action or in thought;
Measure the lot; forgive myself the lot!
When such as I cast out remorse
So great a sweetness flows into the breast
We must laugh and we must sing,   70
We are blest by everything,
Everything we look upon is blest.

Coole Park, 1929

I meditate upon a swallow's flight,
Upon an aged woman and her house,
A sycamore and lime tree lost in night
Although that western cloud is luminous,
Great works constructed there in nature's spite
For scholars and for poets after us,
Thoughts long knitted into a single thought,
A dance-like glory that those walls begot.

There Hyde* before he had beaten into prose
That noble blade the Muses buckled on,   10
There one that ruffled in a manly pose
For all his timid heart, there that slow man,
That meditative man, John Synge,* and those
Impetuous men, Shawe-Taylor and Hugh Lane,*
Found pride established in humility,
A scene well set and excellent company.

They came like swallows and like swallows went,
And yet a woman's powerful character
Could keep a swallow to its first intent;
And half a dozen in formation there,   20
That seemed to whirl upon a compass point,
Found certainty upon the dreaming air,
The intellectual sweetness of those lines
That cut through time or cross it withershins.

Here, traveller, scholar, poet, take your stand
When all those rooms and passages are gone,
When nettles wave upon a shapeless mound
And saplings root among the broken stone,
And dedicate – eyes bent upon the ground,
Back turned upon the brightness of the sun   30
And all the sensuality of the shade –
A moment's memory to that laurelled head.

Coole and Ballylee, 1931

Under my window ledge the waters race,
Otters below and moor hens on the top,
Run for a mile undimmed in Heaven's face
Then darkening through "dark" Raftery's* "cellar" drop,
Run underground, rise in a rocky place
In Coole demesne, and there to finish up
Spread to a lake and drop into a hole.
What's water but the generated soul?

Upon the border of that lake's a wood
Now all dry sticks under a wintry sun,   10
And in a copse of beeches there I stood,
For Nature's pulled her tragic buskin on
And all the rant's a mirror of my mood:
At sudden thunder of the mounting swan
I turned about and looked where branches break
The glittering reaches of the flooded lake.

Another emblem there! That stormy white
But seems a concentration of the sky,
And, like the soul, it sails into the sight
And in the morning's gone, no man knows why,   20
And is so lovely that it sets to right
What knowledge or its lack had set awry,
So arrogantly pure, a child might think
It can be murdered with a spot of ink.

Sound of a stick upon the floor, a sound
From somebody that toils from chair to chair;
Beloved books that famous hands have bound,
Old marble heads, old pictures everywhere;
Great rooms where travelled men and children found
Content or joy; a last inheritor   30
Where none has reigned that lacked a name and fame
Or out of folly into folly came.

89

A spot whereon the founders lived and died
Seemed once more dear than life; ancestral trees
Or gardens rich in memory glorified
Marriages, alliances and families,
And every bride's ambition satisfied.
Where fashion or mere fantasy decrees
Man shifts about – all that great glory spent –
Like some poor Arab tribesman and his tent.   40

We were the last romantics – chose for theme
Traditional sanctity and loveliness;
Whatever's written in what poets name
The book of the people; whatever most can bless
The mind of man or elevate a rhyme,
But all is changed, that high horse riderless,
Though mounted in that saddle Homer rode
Where the swan drifts upon a darkening flood.

Byzantium

The unpurged images of day recede;
The Emperor's drunken soldiery are abed;
Night resonance recedes, night walkers' song
After great cathedral gong;
A starlit or a moonlit dome disdains
All that man is,
All mere complexities,
The fury and the mire of human veins.

Before me floats an image, man or shade,
Shade more than man, more image than a shade;   10
For Hades' bobbin bound in mummy cloth
May unwind the winding path;
A mouth that has no moisture and no breath
Breathless mouths may summon;
I hail the superhuman;
I call it death-in-life and life-in-death.

Miracle, bird or golden handiwork,
More miracle than bird or handiwork,
Planted on the starlit golden bough,
Can like the cocks of Hades crow,   20
Or, by the moon embittered, scorn aloud
In glory of changeless metal
Common bird or petal
And all complexities of mire or blood.

At midnight on the Emperor's pavement flit
Flames that no faggot feeds, nor steel has lit,
Nor storm disturbs, flames begotten of flame,
Where blood-begotten spirits come
And all complexities of fury leave,
Dying into a dance,   30
An agony of trance,
An agony of flame that cannot singe a sleeve.

Astraddle on the dolphin's mire and blood,
Spirit after spirit! The smithies break the flood,
The golden smithies of the Emperor!
Marbles of the dancing floor
Break bitter furies of complexity,
Those images that yet
Fresh images beget,
That dolphin-torn, that gong-tormented sea.   40

Crazy Jane and the Bishop

Bring me to the blasted oak
That I, midnight upon the stroke,
(*All find safety in the tomb.*)
May call down curses on his head
Because of my dear Jack that's dead.
Coxcomb was the least he said:
The solid man and the coxcomb.

Nor was he Bishop when his ban
Banished Jack the Journeyman,
(*All find safety in the tomb.*)   10
Nor so much as parish priest,
Yet he, an old book in his fist,
Cried that we lived like beast and beast:
The solid man and the coxcomb.

The Bishop has a skin, God knows,
Wrinkled like the foot of a goose,
(*All find safety in the tomb.*)
Nor can he hide in holy black
The heron's hunch upon his back,
But a birch tree stood my Jack: 20
The solid man and the coxcomb.

Jack had my virginity,
And bids me to the oak, for he
(*All find safety in the tomb.*)
Wanders out into the night
And there is shelter under it,
But should that other come, I spit:
The solid man and the coxcomb.

Mad as the Mist and Snow

Bolt and bar the shutter,
For the foul winds blow:
Our minds are at their best this night,
And I seem to know
That everything outside us is
Mad as the mist and snow.

Horace* there by Homer stands,
Plato stands below,
And here is Tully's* open page.
How many years ago   10
Were you and I unlettered lads
Mad as the mist and snow?

You ask what makes me sigh, old friend,
What makes me shudder so?
I shudder and I sigh to think
That even Cicero
And many-minded Homer were
Mad as the mist and snow.

Father and Child

She hears me strike the board and say
That she is under ban
Of all good men and women,
Being mentioned with a man
That has the worst of all bad names;
And thereupon replies
That his hair is beautiful,
Cold as the March wind his eyes.

A Prayer for Old Age

God guard me from those thoughts men think
In the mind alone;
He that sings a lasting song
Thinks in a marrow bone;

From all that makes a wise old man
That can be praised of all;
Oh what am I that I should not seem
For the song's sake a fool?

I pray – for fashion's word is out
And prayer comes round again –   10
That I may seem, though I die old,
A foolish, passionate man.

Meru

Civilization is hooped together, brought
Under a rule, under the semblance of peace
By manifold illusion, but man's life is thought,
And he, despite his terror, cannot cease
Ravening through century after century,
Ravening, raging and uprooting that he may come
Into the desolation of reality:
Egypt and Greece, goodbye, and goodbye, Rome!
Hermits upon Mount Meru or Everest,
Caverned in night under the drifted snow,   10
Or where that snow and winter's dreadful blast
Beat down upon their naked bodies, know
That day bring round the night, that before dawn
His glory and his monuments are gone.

The Gyres

The gyres! the gyres! Old Rocky Face,* look forth;
Things thought too long can be no longer thought,
For beauty dies of beauty, worth of worth,
And ancient lineaments are blotted out.
Irrational streams of blood are staining earth;
Empedocles* has thrown all things about;
Hector is dead and there's a light in Troy;
We that look on but laugh in tragic joy.

What matter though numb nightmare ride on top
And blood and mire the sensitive body stain?   10
What matter? Heave no sigh, let no tear drop,
A greater, a more gracious time has gone;
For painted forms or boxes of make-up
In ancient tombs I sighed, but not again;
What matter? Out of Cavern comes a voice
And all it knows is that one word, "Rejoice".

Conduct and work grow coarse, and coarse the soul,
What matter! Those that Rocky Face holds dear,
Lovers of horses and of women, shall,
From marble of a broken sepulchre,   20
Or dark betwixt the polecat and the owl,
Or any rich, dark nothing disinter
The workman, noble and saint, and all things run
On that unfashionable gyre again.

Lapis Lazuli

(For Harry Clifton)*

I have heard that hysterical women say
They are sick of the palette and fiddle bow,
Of poets that are always gay,
For everybody knows or else should know
That if nothing drastic is done
Aeroplane and Zeppelin will come out,
Pitch like King Billy bomb balls in
Until the town lie beaten flat.

All perform their tragic play:
There struts Hamlet, there is Lear,   10
That's Ophelia, that Cordelia;
Yet they, should the last scene be there,
The great stage curtain about to drop,
If worthy their prominent part in the play,
Do not break up their lines to weep.
They know that Hamlet and Lear are gay;
Gaiety transfiguring all that dread.
All men have aimed at, found and lost;
Black out; Heaven blazing into the head:
Tragedy wrought to its uttermost.   20
Though Hamlet rambles and Lear rages,
And all the drop scenes drop at once
Upon a hundred thousand stages,
It cannot grow by an inch or an ounce.

On their own feet they came, or on shipboard,
Camel-back, horse-back, ass-back, mule-back,
Old civilizations put to the sword.
Then they and their wisdom went to rack:
No handiwork of Callimachus,*
Who handled marble as if it were bronze,   30

99

Made draperies that seemed to rise
When sea wind swept the corner, stands;
His long lamp chimney shaped like the stem
Of a slender palm, stood but a day;
All things fall and are built again,
And those that build them again are gay.

Two Chinamen, behind them a third,
Are carved in lapis lazuli,
Over them flies a long-legged bird,
A symbol of longevity;   40
The third, doubtless a serving-man,
Carries a musical instrument.

Every discoloration of the stone,
Every accidental crack or dent,
Seems a water course or an avalanche,
Or lofty slope where it still snows
Though doubtless plum or cherry branch
Sweetens the little halfway house
Those Chinamen climb towards, and I
Delight to imagine them seated there;   50
There, on the mountain and the sky,
On all the tragic scene they stare.
One asks for mournful melodies;
Accomplished fingers begin to play.
Their eyes mid many wrinkles, their eyes,
Their ancient, glittering eyes, are gay.

An Acre of Grass

Picture and book remain,
An acre of green grass
For air and exercise,
Now strength of body goes;
Midnight, an old house
Where nothing stirs but a mouse.

My temptation is quiet.
Here at life's end
Neither loose imagination,
Nor the mill of the mind   10
Consuming its rag and bone
Can make the truth known.

Grant me an old man's frenzy.
Myself must I remake
Till I am Timon and Lear
Or that William Blake
Who beat upon the wall
Till Truth obeyed his call;

A mind Michelangelo knew
That can pierce the clouds   20
Or inspired by frenzy
Shake the dead in their shrouds;
Forgotten else by mankind
An old man's eagle mind.

What Then?

His chosen comrades thought at school
He must grow a famous man;
He thought the same and lived by rule,
All his twenties crammed with toil;
"What then?" sang Plato's ghost. "What then?"

Everything he wrote was read,
After certain years he won
Sufficient money for his need,
Friends that have been friends indeed;
"What then?" sang Plato's ghost. "What then?"   10

All his happier dreams came true –
A small old house, wife, daughter, son,
Grounds where plum and cabbage grew,
Poets and Wits about him drew;
"What then?" sang Plato's ghost. "What then?"

"The work is done," grown old he thought,
"According to my boyish plan;
Let the fools rage, I swerved in naught,
Something to perfection brought."
But louder sang that ghost, "What then?"   20

Beautiful Lofty Things

Beautiful lofty things: O'Leary's* noble head;
My father upon the Abbey stage, before him a raging crowd.
"This Land of Saints," and then as the applause died out,
"Of plaster Saints"; his beautiful mischievous head thrown back.
Standish O'Grady* supporting himself between the tables
Speaking to a drunken audience high nonsensical words;
Augusta Gregory* seated at her great ormolu table,
Her eightieth winter approaching; "Yesterday he threatened my life,
I told him that nightly from six to seven I sat at this table,
The blinds drawn up"; Maud Gonne at Howth station waiting a train,   10
Pallas Athena in that straight back and arrogant head:
All the Olympians; a thing never known again.

The Great Day

Hurrah for revolution and more cannon shot;
A beggar upon horseback lashes a beggar upon foot;
Hurrah for revolution and cannon come again,
The beggars have changed places but the lash goes on.

Parnell

Parnell came down the road, he said to a cheering man:
"Ireland shall get her freedom and you still break stone."

What Was Lost

I sing what was lost and dread what was won,
I walk in a battle fought over again,
My king a lost king, and lost soldiers my men;
Feet to the Rising and Setting may run,
They always beat on the same small stone.

The Spur

You think it horrible that lust and rage
Should dance attendance upon my old age;
They were not such a plague when I was young;
What else have I to spur me into song?

The Old Stone Cross

A statesman is an easy man,
He tells his lies by rote;
A journalist makes up his lies
And takes you by the throat;
So stay at home and drink your beer
And let the neighbours vote,
> *Said the man in the golden breastplate*
> *Under the old stone cross.*

Because this age and the next age
Engender in the ditch,
No man can know a happy man
From any passing wretch;
If Folly link with Elegance
No man knows which is which,
> *Said the man in the golden breastplate*
> *Under the old stone cross.*

But actors lacking music
Do most excite my spleen,
They say it is more human
To shuffle, grunt and groan,
Not knowing what unearthly stuff
Rounds a mighty scene,
> *Said the man in the golden breastplate*
> *Under the old stone cross.*

10

20

The Municipal Gallery Revisited

I

Around me the images of thirty years;
An ambush; pilgrims at the waterside;
Casement* upon trial, half hidden by the bars,
Guarded; Griffith* staring in hysterical pride;
Kevin O'Higgins'* countenance that wears
A gentle questioning look that cannot hide
A soul incapable of remorse or rest;
A revolutionary soldier kneeling to be blessed.

II

An abbot or archbishop with an upraised hand
Blessing the Tricolour. "This is not," I say,   10
"The dead Ireland of my youth, but an Ireland
The poets have imagined, terrible and gay."
Before a woman's portrait suddenly I stand;
Beautiful and gentle in her Venetian way.
I met her all but fifty years ago
For twenty minutes in some studio.

III

Heart-smitten with emotion I sink down,
My heart recovering with covered eyes;
Wherever I had looked I had looked upon
My permanent or impermanent images;   20
Augusta Gregory's son;* her sister's son,
Hugh Lane, "onlie begetter" of all these;
Hazel Lavery* living and dying, that tale
As though some ballad singer had sung it all;

IV

Mancini's* portrait of Augusta Gregory,
"Greatest since Rembrandt," according to John Synge;*
A great ebullient portrait certainly;

But where is the brush that could show anything
Of all that pride and that humility?
And I am in despair that time may bring   30
Approved patterns of women or of men
But not that selfsame excellence again.

V

My medieval knees lack health until they bend,
But in that woman, in that household where
Honour had lived so long, all lacking found.
Childless I thought, "My children may find here
Deep-rooted things," but never foresaw its end,
And now that end has come I have not wept;
No fox can foul the lair the badger swept.

VI

(An image out of Spenser* and the common tongue.)   40
John Synge, I and Augusta Gregory, thought
All that we did, all that we said or sang
Must come from contact with the soil, from that
Contact everything Antaeus-like* grew strong.
We three alone in modern times had brought
Everything down to that sole test again,
Dream of the noble and the beggarman.

VII

And here's John Synge himself, that rooted man
"Forgetting human words", a grave deep face.
You that would judge me do not judge alone   50
This book or that, come to this hallowed place
Where my friends' portraits hang and look thereon;
Ireland's history in their lineaments trace;
Think where man's glory most begins and ends,
And say my glory was I had such friends.

Why Should Not Old Men Be Mad?

Why should not old men be mad?
Some have known a likely lad
That had a sound fly fisher's wrist
Turn to a drunken journalist;
A girl that knew all Dante once
Live to bear children to a dunce;
A Helen of social welfare dream
Climb on a wagonette to scream.
Some think it matter of course that chance
Should starve good men and bad advance,   10
That if their neighbours figured plain,
As though upon a lighted screen,
No single story would they find
Of an unbroken happy mind,
A finish worthy of the start.
Young men know nothing of this sort,
Observant old men know it well;
And when they know what old books tell
And that no better can be had,
Know why an old man should be mad.   20

Under Ben Bulben

I

Swear by what the sages spoke
Round the Mareotic Lake
That the Witch of Atlas knew,
Spoke and set the cocks a-crow.

Swear by those horsemen, by those women
Complexion and form prove superhuman,
That pale, long-visaged company
That airs an immortality
Completeness of their passions won;
Now they ride the wintry dawn   10
Where Ben Bulben sets the scene.

Here's the gist of what they mean.

II

Many times man lives and dies
Between his two eternities,
That of race and that of soul,
And ancient Ireland knew it all.
Whether man die in his bed
Or the rifle knocks him dead,
A brief parting from those dear
Is the worst man has to fear.   20
Though grave-diggers' toil is long,
Sharp their spades, their muscle strong,
They but thrust their buried men
Back in the human mind again.

III

You that Mitchel's prayer have heard
"Send war in our time, O Lord!"
Know that when all words are said

And a man is fighting mad,
Something drops from eyes long blind,
He completes his partial mind,   30
For an instant stands at ease,
Laughs aloud, his heart at peace,
Even the wisest man grows tense
With some sort of violence
Before he can accomplish fate,
Know his work or choose his mate.

IV

Poet and sculptor, do the work,
Nor let the modish painter shirk
What his great forefathers did,
Bring the soul of man to God,   40
Make him fill the cradles right.

Measurement began our might:
Forms a stark Egyptian thought,
Forms that gentler Phidias* wrought.

Michelangelo left a proof
On the Sistine Chapel roof,
Where but half-awakened Adam
Can disturb globe-trotting Madam
Till her bowels are in heat,
Proof that there's a purpose set   50
Before the secret working mind:
Profane perfection of mankind.

Quattrocento put in paint
On backgrounds for a god or saint,
Gardens where a soul's at ease;
Where everything that meets the eye,
Flowers and grass and cloudless sky,
Resemble forms that are, or seem,
When sleepers wake and yet still dream,
And when it's vanished still declare,   60
With only bed and bedstead there,

That heavens had opened.

                              Gyres run on;
When that greater dream had gone
Calvert and Wilson, Blake and Claude,*
Prepared a rest for the people of God,
Palmer's* phrase, but after that
Confusion fell upon our thought.

V

Irish poets, learn your trade,
Sing whatever is well made,
Scorn the sort now growing up   70
All out of shape from toe to top,
Their unremembering hearts and heads
Base-born products of base beds.
Sing the peasantry, and then
Hard-riding country gentlemen,
The holiness of monks, and after
Porter-drinkers' randy laughter;
Sing the lords and ladies gay
That were beaten into the clay
Through seven heroic centuries;   80
Cast your mind on other days
That we in coming days may be
Still the indomitable Irishry.

VI

Under bare Ben Bulben's head
In Drumcliff churchyard Yeats is laid;
An ancestor was rector there
Long years ago; a church stands near,
By the road an ancient cross.
No marble, no conventional phrase;
On limestone quarried near the spot   90
By his command these words are cut:

> *Cast a cold eye*
> *On life, on death.*
> *Horseman, pass by!*

The Statues

Pythagoras planned it. Why did the people stare?
His numbers, though they moved or seemed to move
In marble or in bronze, lacked character.
But boys and girls, pale from the imagined love
Of solitary beds, knew what they were,
That passion could bring character enough,
And pressed at midnight in some public place
Live lips upon a plummet-measured face.

No; greater than Pythagoras, for the men
That with a mallet or a chisel modelled these   10
Calculations that look but casual flesh, put down
All Asiatic vague immensities,
And not the banks of oars that swam upon
The many-headed foam at Salamis.
Europe put off that foam when Phidias*
Gave women dreams and dreams their looking glass.

One image crossed the many-headed, sat
Under the tropic shade, grew round and slow,
No Hamlet thin from eating flies, a fat
Dreamer of the Middle Ages. Empty eyeballs knew   20
That knowledge increases unreality, that
Mirror on mirror mirrored is all the show.
When gong and conch declare the hour to bless
Grimalkin crawls to Buddha's emptiness.

When Pearse* summoned Cuchulain to his side,
What stalked through the Post Office? What intellect,
What calculation, number, measurement, replied?
We Irish, born into that ancient sect
But thrown upon this filthy modern tide
And by its formless spawning fury wrecked,   30
Climb to our proper dark, that we may trace
The lineaments of a plummet-measured face.

A Bronze Head

Here at right of the entrance this bronze head,
Human, superhuman, a bird's round eye,
Everything else withered and mummy-dead.
What great tomb-haunter sweeps the distant sky
(Something may linger there though all else die)
And finds there nothing to make its terror less
*Hysterica passio** of its own emptiness?

No dark tomb-haunter once; her form all full
As though with magnanimity of light,
Yet a most gentle woman; who can tell   10
Which of her forms has shown her substance right?
Or maybe substance can be composite,
Profound McTaggart* thought so, and in a breath
A mouthful held the extreme of life and death.

But even at the starting post, all sleek and new,
I saw the wildness in her and I thought
A vision of terror that it must live through
Had shattered her soul. Propinquity had brought
Imagination to that pitch where it casts out
All that is not itself. I had grown wild   20
And wandered murmuring everywhere, "My child, my child."

Or else I thought her supernatural;
As though a sterner eye looked through her eye
On this foul world in its decline and fall,
On gangling stocks grown great, great stocks run dry,
Ancestral pearls all pitched into a sty,
Heroic reverie mocked by clown and knave,
And wondered what was left for massacre to save.

High Talk

Processions that lack high stilts have nothing that catches the eye.
What if my great-grandad had a pair that were twenty foot high,
And mine were but fifteen foot, no modern stalks upon higher,
Some rogue of the world stole them to patch up a fence or a fire.

Because piebald ponies, led bears, caged lions, make but poor shows,
Because children demand Daddy-long-legs upon his timber toes,
Because women in the upper stories demand a face at the pane
That patching old heels they may shriek, I take to chisel and plane.
Malachi Stilt-Jack am I, whatever I learned has run wild,
From collar to collar, from stilt to stilt, from father to child.   10

All metaphor, Malachi, stilts and all. A barnacle goose
Far up in the stretches of night; night splits and the dawn breaks loose;
I, through the terrible novelty of light, stalk on, stalk on;
Those great sea-horses bare their teeth and laugh at the dawn.

Man and the Echo

Man

In a cleft that's christened Alt
Under broken stone I halt
At the bottom of a pit
That broad noon has never lit,
And shout a secret to the stone.
All that I have said and done,
Now that I am old and ill,
Turns into a question till
I lie awake night after night
And never get the answers right.   10
Did that play of mine send out
Certain men the English shot?
Did words of mine put too great strain
On that woman's reeling brain?
Could my spoken words have checked
That whereby a house lay wrecked?
And all seems evil until I
Sleepless would lie down and die.

Echo

Lie down and die.

Man

             That were to shirk
The spiritual intellect's great work   20
And shirk it in vain. There is no release
In a bodkin or disease,
Nor can there be a work so great
As that which cleans man's dirty slate.
While man can still his body keep
Wine or love drug him to sleep,
Waking he thanks the Lord that he
Has body and its stupidity,

But body gone he sleeps no more
And till his intellect grows sure   30
That all's arranged in one clear view
Pursues the thoughts that I pursue,
Then stands in judgement on his soul,
And, all work done, dismisses all
Out of intellect and sight
And sinks at last into the night.

Echo
Into the night.

Man
O rocky voice
Shall we in that great night rejoice?
What do we know but that we face
One another in this place?   40
But hush, for I have lost the theme,
Its joy or night seem but a dream;
Up there some hawk or owl has struck
Dropping out of sky or rock,
A stricken rabbit is crying out
And its cry distracts my thought.

The Circus Animals' Desertion

I

I sought a theme and sought for it in vain,
I sought it daily for six weeks or so.
Maybe at last being but a broken man
I must be satisfied with my heart, although
Winter and summer till old age began
My circus animals were all on show,
Those stilted boys, that burnished chariot,
Lion and woman and the Lord knows what.

II

What can I but enumerate old themes,
First that sea-rider Oisin* led by the nose   10
Through three enchanted islands, allegorical dreams,
Vain gaiety, vain battle, vain repose,
Themes of the embittered heart, or so it seems,
That might adorn old songs or courtly shows,
But what cared I that set him on to ride,
I, starved for the bosom of his fairy bride.

And then a counter-truth filled out its play,
*The Countess Cathleen** was the name I gave it;
She, pity-crazed, had given her soul away
But masterful Heaven had intervened to save it.   20
I thought my dear must her own soul destroy
So did fanaticism and hate enslave it,
And this brought forth a dream and soon enough
This dream itself had all my thought and love.

And when the Fool and Blind Man stole the bread
Cuchulain fought the ungovernable sea;*
Heart mysteries there, and yet when all is said
It was the dream itself enchanted me:
Character isolated by a deed

120

To engross the present and dominate memory.   30
Players and painted stage took all my love
And not those things that they were emblems of.

III

Those masterful images because complete
Grew in pure mind, but out of what began?
A mound of refuse or the sweepings of a street,
Old kettles, old bottles and a broken can,
Old iron, old bones, old rags, that raving slut
Who keeps the till. Now that my ladder's gone,
I must lie down where all the ladders start
In the foul rag-and-bone shop of the heart.   40

Note on the Text

The title of each poem is followed by the date of its first publication. *The Song of the Happy Shepherd* (1885). *Down by the Salley Gardens* (1889). *The Meditation of the Old Fisherman* (1886). *Cuchulain's Fight with the Sea* (1892). *When You Are Old* (1892). *The Lamentation of the Old Pensioner* (1890, although the version reproduced here is a revision of the poem that Yeats produced in 1925). *He Wishes for the Cloths of Heaven* (1899). *Never Give All the Heart* (1905). *Adam's Curse* (1902). *The Old Men Admiring Themselves in the Water* (1903). *Words* (1910). *Peace* (1910). *The Fascination of What's Difficult* (1910). *Upon a House Shaken by the Land Agitation* (1910). *These Are the Clouds* (1910). *At Galway Races* (1909). *All Things Can Tempt Me* (1909). *To a Wealthy Man Who Promised a Second Subscription to the Dublin Municipal Gallery if it Were Proved the People Wanted Pictures* (1913). *September 1913* (1913). *When Helen Lived* (1914). *Fallen Majesty* (1912). *Friends* (1912). *That the Night Come* (1912). *A Coat* (1914). *While I, from That Reed-throated Whisperer...* (1914). *In Memory of Major Robert Gregory* (1918). *An Irish Airman Foresees His Death* (1919). *To a Young Beauty* (1918). *The Scholars* (1915). *Her Praise* (1916). *Broken Dreams* (1917). *Ego Dominus Tuus* (1917). *Easter, 1916* (1917). *Sixteen Dead Men* (1920). *The Rose Tree* (1920). *On a Political Prisoner* (1920). *The Second Coming* (1920). *A Prayer for my Daughter* (1919). *Sailing to Byzantium* (1927). *The Tower* (1927). *Meditations in Time of Civil War* (1923). *Nineteen Hundred and Nineteen* (1921). *Two Songs from a Play* (1927, apart from the second stanza of the second song, which was first published in 1931). *Leda and the Swan* (1924). *Among School Children* (1927). *All Souls' Night* (1921). *In Memory of Eva Gore-Booth and Con Markiewicz* (1929). *A Dialogue of Self and Soul* (1929). *Coole Park, 1929* (1931). *Coole and Ballylee, 1931* (1932). *Byzantium* (1932). *Crazy Jane and the Bishop* (1930). *Mad as the Mist and Snow* (1932). *Father and Child* (1929). *A Prayer for Old Age* (1934). *Meru* (1934). *The Gyres* (1938). *Lapis Lazuli* (1938). *An Acre of Grass* (1938). *What Then?* (1937). *Beautiful Lofty Things* (1938). *The Great Day* (1938). *Parnell* (1938). *What Was Lost* (1938). *The Spur* (1938). *The Old Stone Cross* (1938). *The Municipal Gallery Revisited* (1937). *Why Should Not Old Men Be Mad?* (1939). *Under Ben Bulben* (1939). *The Statues* (1939). *A Bronze Head* (1939). *High Talk* (1938). *Man and the Echo* (1939). *The Circus Animals' Desertion* (1939).

Notes

p. 3, *Chronos*: The personification of time in Greek mythology.

p. 24, *Paudeen's*: A "Paudeen" means a plebeian.

p. 24, *Duke Ercole*: Ercole d'Este (1431–1505), Duke of Ferrara and patron of the arts.

p. 24, *Plautus*: Titus Maccius Plautus (c.254–184 BC), Roman playwright.

p. 24, *Guidobaldo*: Guidobaldo di Montefeltro (1472–1508), Duke of Urbino.

p. 24, *Cosimo*: Cosimo de' Medici (1384–1464), Florentine patron of the arts.

p. 24, *Michelozzo's*: Michelozzo di Bartolomeo Michelozzi (1396–1472), Florentine architect.

p. 26, *O'Leary*: John O'Leary (1830–1907), Fenian leader whom Yeats admired.

p. 26, *wild geese*: Irish soldiers who left the country to serve in continental European armies.

p. 26, *Edward Fitzgerald*: Lord Edward Fitzgerald (1763–98), Irish revolutionary; he died in the 1798 uprising.

p. 26, *Robert Emmet*: Robert Emmett (1778–1803), Irish patriot; he led the 1803 revolt against England, and was captured and executed.

p. 26, *Wolfe Tone*: Theobald Wolfe Tone (1763–98), Irish revolutionary, the father of Irish republicanism.

p. 33, *Major Robert Gregory*: Robert Gregory (1881–1918) was the son of Lady Augusta Gregory (1852–1932). A talented scholar and artist, he died fighting in Italy.

p. 33, *Lionel Johnson*: Lionel Pigot Johnson (1867–1902), the English poet and critic; he was acquainted with Yeats through the Rhymers' Club, the poetry group which they were both members of.

p. 33, *John Synge*: Edmund John Millington Synge (1871–1909), Irish playwright; together with Yeats and others, he cofounded the Irish Literary Theatre (later known as the Abbey Theatre).

p. 34, *George Pollexfen*: George Pollexfen (1839–1910) was Yeats's uncle on his mother's side.

p. 34, *Sidney*: A reference to Sir Philip Sidney (1554–86), the Elizabethan poet, who died fighting in Holland.

p. 38, *Ezekiel's cherubim*: See Ezekiel 10.

p. 38, *Beauvarlet*: Jacques Beauvarlet (1731–97), French painter.

p. 38, *Landor*: Walter Savage Landor (1775–1864), English poet.

p. 39, *Catullus*: Gaius Valerius Catullus (*c*.84 BC–*c*.54 BC), Roman poet.

p. 43, *Ego Dominus Tuus*: "I am your lord" (Latin).

p. 43, *Hic*: "This one" (Latin).

p. 43, *Michael Robartes*: Not an actual historical personage, the figure of Michael Robartes occurs in a number of Yeats's poems, with a metaphorical and occult significance.

p. 43, *Ille*: "That one" (Latin).

p. 43, *Lapo... Guido*: Lapo is possibly Lapo Gianni; Guido is Guido Cavalcanti (1230–1300), Italian poet and friend of Dante's; both are referred to in a famous sonnet of Dante's addressed to Cavalcanti.

p. 48, *MacDonagh... MacBride... Connolly... Pearse*: Thomas Mac-Donagh (1878–1916); John MacBride (1868–1916), husband to Maud Gonne; James Connolly (1870–1916); and Patrick Pearse (1879–1916) were all executed by the British for their roles in the Easter Rising of 1916, which attempted to establish an Irish Republic.

p. 49, *Pearse*: See note to page 48.

p. 49, *MacDonagh's*: See note to page 48.

p. 49, *Lord Edward and Wolfe Tone*: See third and fifth notes to page 26 respectively.

p. 50, *Pearse... Connolly*: See note to page 48.

p. 52, *Spiritus Mundi*: "The soul of the world" (Latin).

p. 53, *that great Queen*: Venus.

p. 53, *bandy-leggèd smith*: Vulcan, Venus's husband.

p. 58, *Plotinus*: Plotinus (205–70 AD), Neoplatonic philosopher.

p. 58, *Mrs French*: An Irish grandee described by historian Sir Jonah Barrington in his book *Recollections*.

p. 59, *Hanrahan*: A fictional poet.

p. 62, *Burke... Grattan*: Edmund Burke (1729–97), politician and philosopher; Henry Grattan (1746–1820), politician.

p. 65, *Il Penseroso's Platonist*: A reference to the poet John Milton (1608–74), the author of *Il Penseroso* (1631).

p. 66, *Sato's... sword*: A reference to a sword given to Yeats by a Japanese man.

p. 68, *Irregular*: A member of the IRA.

p. 68, *brown Lieutenant*: A member of the National Army.

p. 69, *Jacques Molay*: Jacques de Molay (1243–1314), the last grand master of the Knights Templar.

p. 74, *Herodias'*: Herodias (*d.* 39 AD), the wife of Herod Antipas, tetrarch of Galilee from 4 BC to 39 AD. Her daughter's dance led to the execution of John the Baptist.

p. 74, *Robert Artisson*: An evil spirit.

p. 74, *Lady Kyteler*: Dame Alice Kyteler, a fourteenth-century witch.

p. 75, *Magnus Annus*: "The great year" (Latin).

p. 81, *Horton's*: William Thomas Horton (1864–1919), painter.

p. 82, *Florence Emery*: Florence Farr Emery (1869–1917), English actress.

p. 82, *MacGregor Mathers*: MacGregor Mathers (1854–1918), leader in the Order of the Golden Dawn, an occult society to which Yeats belonged.

p. 84, *Eva Gore-Booth and Con Markiewicz*: Eva Selina Laura Gore-Booth (1870–1926) was an Irish poet and dramatist, and her older sister, Constance Gore-Booth Markiewicz (1868–1927), was an Irish revolutionary nationalist and politician.

p. 84, *Lissadell*: The family home of the Gore-Booths.

p. 85, *Sato's ancient blade*: See note to page 66.

p. 88, *Hyde*: Dr Douglas Hyde (1860–1949), poet and statesman.

p. 88, *John Synge*: See third note to page 33.

p. 88, *Shawe-Taylor and Hugh Lane*: Lady Augusta Gregory's nephews.

p. 89, *Raftery's*: Anthony Raftery was a local Gaelic poet.

p. 94, *Horace*: Horace (65–8 BC), the Roman poet.

p. 94, *Tully's*: Marcus Tullius Cicero (106–43 BC), the Roman philosopher and rhetorician.

p. 98, *Rocky Face*: A reference to the Delphic oracle.

p. 98, *Empedocles*: Empedocles (*c.*493–*c.*433 BC), the pre-Socratic philosopher.

p. 99, *Harry Clifton*: A young poet who gave Yeats a lapis lazuli carving as a present.

p. 99, *Callimachus*: Fifth-century BC Greek sculptor.

p. 103, *O'Leary's*: See first note to page 26.

p. 103, *Standish O'Grady*: Standish James O'Grady (1846–1928), Irish historian and scholar.

p. 103, *Augusta Gregory*: Lady Augusta Gregory (1852–1932), Irish dramatist, folklorist and friend of Yeats's.

p. 109, *Casement*: Sir Roger Casement (1864–1916), Irish revolutionary captured and hanged for treason by the British.

p. 109, *Griffith*: Arthur Griffith (1871–1922), founder of Sinn Féin.

p. 109, *Kevin O'Higgins'*: Kevin O'Higgins (1892–1927), Minister for Justice of the Irish Free State.

p. 109, *Augusta Gregory's son*: See first note to page 33.

p. 109, *Hazel Lavery*: Lady Hazel Lavery (1880–1935), artist and second wife of Sir John Lavery, the famous portrait artist.

p. 109, *Mancini's*: Antonio Mancini (1852–1930), Italian painter.

p. 109, *John Synge*: See third note to page 33.

p. 110, *Spenser*: Edmund Spenser (*c*.1552–99), Elizabethan poet.

p. 110, *Antaeus*: Antaeus was the giant fought by Hercules, who remained incredibly strong as long as he remained in touch with the ground.

p. 113, *Phidias*: Phidias (fl. *c*.490–430 BC), Greek sculptor.

p. 114, *Calvert and Wilson... Claude*: Edward Calvert (1799–1883), English painter; Richard Wilson (1714–82), Welsh landscape painter, or Yeats may have meant to refer to George Wilson (1848–90), a painter who was friends with his father; Claude Gellée (1600–82), also known as Claude Lorrain, French landscape painter.

p. 114, *Palmer's*: Samuel Palmer (1805–81), English painter.

p. 115, *Phidias*: See note to page 113.

p. 115, *Pearse*: See note to page 48.

p. 116, *Hysterica passio*: "Hysterical passion" – see *King Lear*, Act II, Sc. 4, l. 57.

p. 116, *McTaggart*: J.M.E. McTaggart (1866–1925), British Idealist philosopher.

p. 120, *Oisin*: A reference to Yeats's first major work, *The Wanderings of Oisin* (1889).

p. 120, *The Countess Cathleen*: The title of a play by Yeats.

p. 120, *the Fool and Blind Man... Cuchulain... sea*: References to Yeats's 1904 play *On Baile's Strand*.

Extra Material

on

W.B. Yeats's

Selected Poems

W.B. Yeats's Life

William Butler Yeats was born on 13th June 1865 at 1 George's Ville (now 5 Sandymount Avenue), Dublin, to John Butler Yeats (1839–1922) and Susan Mary, née Pollexfen (1841–1900). John Yeats was a barrister at the time of William's birth, though soon afterwards he gave up law in favour of a career as a portrait painter. The couple went on to have three more children: Susan Mary Yeats, Elizabeth Corbet Yeats and John Butler Yeats. All of the children would go on to be successful in artistic fields, with John Butler Yeats (also known as Jack Butler Yeats) becoming a painter of significant stature. *Birth and Background*

The Yeats family was part of the "Protestant Ascendancy" – a phrase referring to the domination of Ireland by a minority belonging to the Church of Ireland and Church of England since the seventeenth century, even though most of the country was Catholic. By the time William was born, however, this domination was slipping due to the nationalist revival of the late nineteenth century. Ireland's political situation was a great influence on William's writing, as he sought to cultivate a new kind of national identity.

In 1867 the family moved to London to further John's new career as an artist, although Yeats and his siblings continued to spend long intervals with their grandparents in Sligo in western Ireland, where their mother came from. This setting influenced Yeats deeply – he drew on its scenery, folklore and legends in his later writing. From 1877 onwards Yeats attended the Godolphin school in Hammersmith in London, where he did not distinguish himself academically, but the family moved back to Dublin in 1881. He finished his schooling in Dublin at the Erasmus Smith high school, before attending the Metropolitan School of Art from 1883 to 1885. By this *Stays in London and Education* time, Yeats was starting to write – two short lyrics by him were published in the *Dublin University Review* in 1885. The family moved back to London two years later.

Involvement in Esoteric and Literary Circles Naturally inclined towards an interest in esoteric knowledge, Yeats became interested in mysticism and the occult. In 1890, he was initiated into the Hermetic Order of the Golden Dawn. He intensively studied the prophetic books of William Blake, which led him on to looking into Platonism, Neoplatonism, Swedenborg and alchemy. At the same time, he became involved in the literary scene of London, becoming friends with William Morris and W.E. Henley, and cofounding the Rhymers' Club, a poetry group, with Ernest Rhys.

Maud Gonne and Irish Nationalism According to his own reckoning, Yeats met the beautiful ardent Irish nationalist Maud Gonne on 30th January 1889 at his family's house, although by her account they had actually met already. William developed an obsessive infatuation with her, which was unrequited. He proposed marriage to her in 1891. She rejected him, and he later wrote that it was then that "the troubling of my life began". He proposed to her repeatedly as the years went by, but she turned him down each time. Although she was uninterested in him romantically, they became close friends. She admired his poetry, and they shared interests in the occult and mysticism, telling each other about visions of previous lives, and at one stage achieving – at least according to Yeats – a mystic marriage. William believed that she was consecrated to Ireland – and in a way for him, she was like a personification of Ireland – and his obsessive feelings for her provided part of the motivation for his involvement in Irish nationalism at this time, which was also inspired by the Fenian leader John O'Leary.

Lady Gregory In 1893, Yeats wrote *The Celtic Twilight*, a collection of prose pieces exploring the world of Irish folklore, which contributed to the movement of Celtic revivalism. Three years later, he met and became friends with Lady Augusta Gregory, who was also interested in Irish folklore, and Yeats began to spend his summers at her home in Coole Park. Yeats's relationship to Lady Gregory was a great source of strength to him, and had a significant impact on his life. Their mutual interest in drama encouraged him to focus on writing plays, which he did for the next decade.

The nationalists decided to celebrate the anniversary of the Irish Rebellion of 1798, and Yeats became involved in the Fenian politics surrounding this, which Maud Gonne was at the centre of. He had hopes at the time that Maud Gonne might finally unite with him romantically, but unfortunately for him this failed to materialize, and instead Maud Gonne told him about a secret affair of hers in Paris which had resulted in children, and was her reason why she could never marry him.

Together with Lady Gregory and others, Yeats founded the Irish Literary Theatre (now known as the Abbey Theatre), for the purpose of performing Celtic and Irish plays. It gave its first performance in Dublin in 1899, of Yeats's own play, *The Countess Cathleen*. He continued to contribute many plays to the Irish Literary Theatre, although other playwrights wrote for it as well – most notably John Millington Synge. He also remained a director of the theatre until the end of his life. *Irish Literary Theatre*

In 1911, Yeats met the American poet Ezra Pound, an admirer of his work, and the two men spent a few winters together studying poetry, with Pound acting as Yeats's secretary and amanuensis. Yeats's poetry underwent a change, his new poetic voice emerging most distinctly in *Responsibilities*, published in 1914. Gone was the Pre-Raphaelite influence of his early verse, and its other-worldly atmosphere, and a new directness and concision were adopted. Pound also introduced Yeats to Japanese Noh plays, which he had been translating, and these became an influence on Yeats's own dramatic works. *Ezra Pound and a New Literary Direction*

Around this time, Yeats and Maud Gonne briefly became lovers. Maud Gonne had previously married John MacBride in 1903, leaving Yeats devastated. But they had separated soon afterwards, and MacBride was later executed by firing squad for his part in the 1916 Easter Rising. However, Yeats and Maud soon reverted to her preferred option of a platonic relationship. *Brief Romantic Involvement with Maud Gonne*

In 1917, after having been turned down by Maud Gonne's daughter Iseult, Yeats proposed to Bertha Georgie Hyde-Lees, who accepted him. The marriage was successful, and produced two children: Anne and Michael. In the same year, Yeats published the poetry collection *The Wild Swans at Coole*. In this work, and the ones that followed, including *The Tower* (1928) and *The Winding Stair* (1929), many critics have seen him as reaching the summit of his poetic achievement. In 1925, he published *A Vision*, a prose work in which he explained his thinking about the human personality and the course of history by means of a system based upon the phases of the moon. *Marriage and Literary Maturity*

Yeats became a member of the Irish Senate in 1922. He served in it for five years before ill health obliged him to retire.

131

Yeats was awarded the Nobel Prize for Literature in 1923. The prize money and resulting increase in book sales greatly improved his finances, and he used the occasion as a platform to promote recent Irish independence. Unusually for a Nobel Prize winner, the work he produced after winning the prize is often seen by critics as superior to his previous work.

Ill Health and Death   By the 1930s, Yeats's health was failing. Nevertheless, he continued to write and remained engaged in political issues. At this time, he was losing faith in democracy, and seems to have been drawn towards elements of Fascism, without going as far as his friend Ezra Pound, and there is no record of his being anti-Semitic. The condition of Yeats's health made a stay in the south of France necessary in 1938. On 28th January 1939, he died at Roquebrune.

Yeats wanted to be buried back in Sligo in Ireland, but the outbreak of the Second World War meant that it was nine years before his wish could be honoured. In 1948, his coffin was brought back to Ireland, and on 17th September 1948, he was buried in Drumcliff churchyard, Sligo.

Editor's Note

In one of his earliest poems Yeats asserts that

> Words alone are certain good.
> ('The Song of the Happy Shepherd')

And in one of his last poems he again stresses the over-riding importance to him of his art:

> Players and painted stage took all my love
> And not those things that they were emblems of.
> ('The Circus Animals' Desertion')

The years between, in his life and in his work, can be seen as a struggle between his poetry and everything else. These matters – the history of Ireland in a crucial period, his interest in the paranormal, his various friends (whom he cultivated carefully), his enemies (whom he cultivated just as carefully), his late-established but important marriage and family life – have been discussed by many people at great length and will continue to be discussed, to the great advantage of his readers. To concentrate for these few pages on the style of his poetry is not to deny the importance of the substance, any more than Yeats himself did. Simply, a better understanding of the style leads to greater enjoyment and to a greater understanding of the substance.

In an exceptionally long writing life, which stretched from the late nineteenth century when Victorian England was in its heyday to just before the outbreak of the Second World War, his poetry naturally changes, but with the hindsight of the twenty-first century the continuities are obvious. It would be a pity if concentration on the later poems were to lead, as it sometimes does, to any disparagement of the earlier ones, which are so accomplished.

Yeats lived through the Modernist invasion of England in the early twentieth century, and the partial reaction against it on the part of Auden and his many followers, so it is useful to relate his work to some of Modernism's principal features. The differences are obvious. The breaking up of sentence structures, which is so striking at times in T.S. Eliot (in say 'The Hollow Men' or 'Ash Wednesday') and which continues throughout Pound's *Cantos*, is not to be found in Yeats. On the contrary he praises what he called 'natural momentum in the syntax'. As with any stylistic choice, this is also a psychological and moral matter:

> All perform their tragic play,
> There struts Hamlet, there is Lear,
> That's Ophelia, that Cordelia;
> Yet they, should the last scene be there,
> The great stage curtain about to drop,
> If worthy their prominent part in the play,
> Do not break up their lines to weep.
> ('Lapis Lazuli')

Nowadays poets may be praised for a little roughness in the writing, the opinion being apparently that this shows strong emotion and "sincerity". *Chacun à son goût*, of course, but anyone who thinks this way will find much to object to in Yeats and his artistry. A similar feature which came in with Modernism, and which survives to the present day despite the influence of W.H. Auden, is what is known as free verse. Yeats, who was well aware of other fashions, stuck to strict verse forms. One variation of his (not his invention but something he brought into common use) is the employment of half-rhymes (which depend on the identity of the final consonants only of words). This was a truly liberating measure: English is poor in rhymes, but half-rhymes broaden the possibilities, as in:

> Because this age and the next age
> Engender in the ditch,
> No man can know a happy man
> From any passing wretch.
> If Folly link with Elegance
> No man knows which is which...
> ('The Old Stone Cross')

Or

> Did that play of mine send out
> Certain men the English shot?
> ('Man and the Echo')

In that second quotation the dissonance between the rhyme words helps to emphasize "shot", as also does the slight pause before that word enforced by the repetition of the "sh" sound. This use of half-rhymes, which is seldom commented on, is far more important and influential than Wilfred Owen's celebrated use of pararhymes, since the latter are too thin on the ground to be in common use.

It is not unusual for poems to be praised because they "successfully resist closure", meaning apparently that they do not come to any firm conclusion (the implication being that, if they followed their natural impulses, poems would finish themselves neatly). But Yeats enjoys rounding his poems off resoundingly:

> And dedicate – eyes bent upon the ground,
> Back turned upon the brightness of the sun
> And all the sensuality of the shade –
> A moment's memory to that laurelled head.
> ('Coole Park, 1929')

The impression is usually that the last word has been said. Many of his poems end with a question which makes a strong conclusion:

How can we know the dancer from the dance?
('Among School Children')

The movement known as Imagism, short-lived as it was bound to be, nevertheless was not only in at the birth of Modernism, but has continued to be influential since. Concrete images are in, abstractions are out – or so it often seems. The reader is presented with an image and left to work out its meaning, with different results for different readers. Even in a poem which is, for him, quite explicit at times, Eliot does drop in lines which are concrete enough for anyone, but which baffle understanding:

Garlic and sapphires in the mud
Clot the bedded axle-tree.
('Burnt Norton')

Such images always find interpreters – just as there were wonder-workers once who were said to understand the language of birds – but the interpreters do find it hard to agree with each other, and the reader is left with the responsibility to complete a half-written poem. This can happen with Yeats, but he clearly does not wish it. On the contrary, he does at times work a gloss into the poem itself to help the reader along:

What's water but the generated soul?
('Coole Park and Ballylee, 1931')

or (in reference to Sato's sword)

Montashigi, third of his family, fashioned it
Five hundred years ago, about it lie
Flowers from I know not what embroidery –
Heart's purple – and all these I set
For emblems of the day against the tower
Emblematical of the night...
('A Dialogue of Self and Soul')

One of the best ways to understand one poem of Yeats is to read another. A reading of 'A Prayer for my Daughter', which is among his greatest achievements, is helped by an acquaintance with, say, 'Coole Park and Ballylee, 1931', the sections 'My House' and 'My Descendants' from 'Meditations in Time of

Civil War', 'The Second Coming', 'When Helen Lived', 'Why Should Not Old Men Be Mad?', or any of the many poems which allude to Maud Gonne. The fact that four out of those six poems named were written later than 'A Prayer for my Daughter' shows how fortunate the reader is to have access to the whole of Yeats's work. This is not to say that Yeats cannot be obscure. He sometimes appears to be referring to something we should apparently know about, but may not. In 'Ego Dominus Tuus' the source of the title is readily ascertained, but we may well be mystified by his description of Dante, who was

> Derided and deriding, driven out
> To climb that stair and eat that bitter bread.

The reader, feeling that he is missing something, yet intoxicated by the words, is likely to wonder, in Yeatsian mode: "What stair? What bitter bread?" The demonstrative adjectives suggest we ought to know. The ultimate source is in Dante's *Paradiso*, where his ancestor Cacciaguida warns him of the coming exile:

> Tu proverai sì come sa di sale
> lo pane altrui, e come è duro calle
> lo scendere e 'l salir per l'altrui scale.
> (XVII: 58–60)
> (You shall experience how bitter is the taste of another's bread, and how hard it is to have to go up and down another's stairs.)

Yeats knew no language but English, yet curiously it seems that his fondness for the word "bitter" has enabled him to translate "*sa di sale*" more accurately than the two translators (Carey and Shadwell) he usually relied upon and several other more recent and well-known ones. There is then plenty of scope in Yeats for scholars to pursue their interests. And it must be admitted that there are times when "a fine bit of talk" (in John Synge's phrase) appears to have the edge on clarity:

> That dolphin-torn, that gong-tormented sea.
> ('Byzantium')

Obscurity is perhaps hard for any poet in a culture with a historically and internationally wide sphere of reference to avoid entirely. I suggest that Yeats is commonly less obscure than other famous and fashionable poets like Hölderlin, Eliot and Rilke, and he does often, somewhere in his voluminous writings, explain himself.

A common cause of obscurity is the scattering of concrete images without a verbal link provided by the poet. This simply does not occur with Yeats, whose poems are always energetic and eloquent: the sentence carries the reader along with it. Eloquence is not a word often applied now to poets; it tends rather to be associated with speech-making. However, eloquence does work in accordance with the nature of the medium of words. Poetry is a verbal art whose natural tendency is to move through time, unlike the plastic arts. And this is not just a matter of words representing physical movement:

> The Assyrian came down like the wolf on the fold,
> And his cohorts were gleaming in purple and gold;
> And the sheen of their spears was like stars on the sea
> When the blue wave rolls nightly on deep Galilee.
> (Byron, 'The Destruction of Sennacherib')

The words here move rapidly, but the thought and the mood do not; in fact, they are immobile. In this one respect it is reminiscent of

> Up the airy mountain,
>   Down the rushy glen,
> We daren't go a-hunting
>   For fear of little men;
> Wee folk, good folk,
>   Trooping all together;
> Green jacket, red cap,
>   And white owl's feather!
> (William Allingham, 'The Fairies')

We can contrast a passage of Yeats, not one of his best but typical of his procedure:

> Mancini's portrait of Augusta Gregory,
> 'Greatest since Rembrandt,' according to John Synge;

A great ebullient portrait certainly;
But where is the brush that could show anything
Of all that pride and that humility,
And I am in despair that time may bring
Approved patterns of women and of men
But not that selfsame excellence again.
('The Municipal Gallery Re-visited')

The first line announces the theme; the second line appears to praise the painting, but the phrase "according to John Synge" suggests some reservation; the third line suggests an even more restrained appreciation of the painting, with a slight touch of humour: finally the fourth line and those that follow move from the painting to its subject, by whom the writer is swept away in admiration. There is a development of thought, with several changes of tone, within the space of a few lines. The stanza does not in the end leave our minds in the same place where they started. This sort of energy is everywhere in Yeats. An apparently simple poem like 'Mad as the Mist and Snow', described by Yeats himself as a "mechanical little song", shows a similar variation of mood and meaning within the short space of eighteen lines. And as often happens, one carefully placed word can make all the difference, as in the poem's conclusion:

I shudder and I sigh to think
That even Cicero
And many-minded Homer were
Mad as the mist and snow.

Much virtue, and much humour, in that word "even".

Since none of the poems in this selection could be described simply as a "humorous poem", it is worth dwelling on the part humour plays in them. It arrives usually when least expected, and the surprise which it occasions has the effect of making us pause to see things from a slightly different angle. The humour is an aspect of the extravagance which Yeats loved in his writing, while at the same time it qualifies any extravagance in what is said. It is on a par with his delight, in his mature poems, in colloquial words and phrases which do not destroy the high style but somehow strengthen it:

> Winter and summer till old age began
> My circus animals were all on show,
> Those stilted boys, that burnished chariot,
> Lion and woman and the Lord knows what.
> ('The Circus Animals' Desertion')

That final phrase conveys the tone admirably. And what about "stilted"? A glance at the first line of 'High Talk'

> Processions that lack high stilts have nothing that catches
> the eye

provides an immediate reference, but the more general meaning ("stiff and pompous") is suggested too. The fleeting smile, the sudden colloquialism, are part of a pervading sense of aristocratic insouciance and easy command of language by which the poems embody the values they extol. The Italians have a word for this combination of skill and nonchalance – *sprezzatura*. It is frequent in Yeats's mature poems, but the ideal was there early on:

> A line will take us hours maybe;
> Yet if it does not seem a moment's thought,
> Our stitching and unstitching has been nought.
> ('Adam's Curse')

The aristocratic style is one with the expression of elitist opinions. Here is a fair instance:

> Guidobaldo, when he made
> That grammar school of courtesies
> Where wit and beauty learned their trade
> Upon Urbino's windy hill,
> Had sent no runners to and fro
> That he might learn the shepherds' will.
> ('To a Wealthy Man')

The touch of irony in the word "trade" is at one with the sentiment. Yeats was certainly no democrat. But then neither was Virgil or Dante or the anonymous author of *Beowulf.* The difference is that those authors lived in times when the modern conception of democracy had not even been thought of, while

139

Yeats knew that he was in many ways pitting himself against the trend of the age. If this is offensive – and there is no doubt that many people find it so – then perhaps such opinions will seem less offensive as time goes on and the burning issues that gave rise to them move further and further into the past, while the style remains fresh, well-seasoned as it is with Attic salt. Yeats was deeply and openly involved in matters that aroused, and can still arouse, violent reactions – "the seeming needs of my fool-driven land", his lifelong enthusiasm for the paranormal, his contempt for hoi polloi, even his flirtation with the idea of selective breeding for human beings – one could go on. As W.H. Auden wrote, in his elegy on Yeats:

> [Time] Worships language and forgives
> Everyone by whom it lives...
> Time that with this strange excuse
> Pardoned Kipling and his views,
> And will pardon Paul Claudel,
> Pardons him for writing well.

These lines were later omitted from the elegy, and do not appear in the definitive text. Perhaps Auden came to regret the patronizing tone, and not the sentiment.

Yeats's poems are crowded with lines where such objections to "political correctness" cannot arise, where the rightness of the expression triumphs without upsetting anyone, since the themes are age-old ones to which we can all respond. There is

> a tale that she
> Told of a harsh reproof, or trivial event
> That changed some childish day to tragedy.
> ('Among School Children')

In that same poem there is the comment on old age:

> Better to smile on all that smile, and show
> There is a comfortable kind of old scarecrow.

A few lines later this becomes

> Old clothes upon old sticks to scare a bird.

There is a quieter, but pithy, description of old age:

> the wreck of body,
> Slow decay of blood,
> Testy delirium
> Or dull decrepitude.
> ('The Tower')

Or the eeriness of physical decay, which in its context is a hint of coming social decay:

> Sound of a stick upon the floor, a sound
> From somebody that toils from chair to chair.
> ('Coole Park and Ballylee, 1931')

Or, in laudatory mood, a description of Maud Gonne:

> But even at the starting post, all sleek and new,
> I saw the wildness in her...
> ('A Bronze Head')

Another age and culture could make a similar comparison explicitly:

> I have compared thee, O my love, to a company of horses in
> Pharaoh's chariots.
> (Song of Solomon 1:9)

In Yeats the comparison is implicit and, with superb tact and restraint, all unwanted connotations are suppressed. And there are many other memorable lines and images in poems which are most striking for their wholeness and completeness.

It is now a lifetime since Yeats died. Not only is he the finest poet of his age, but his poetry has not been equalled since.

– J.G. Nichols

Select Bibliography

Yeats's Poetry

W.B. Yeats. *The Poems,* ed. Daniel Albright (London: Everyman's Library, 1992)

A. Norman Jeffares, *A New Commentary on the Poems of W.B. Yeats* (London: Macmillan, 1984)

In Excited Reverie. A Centenary Tribute to W.B. Yeats, ed. A. Norman Jeffares and K.G.W. Cross (London: Macmillan, and New York: St Martin's Press, 1965)

Other Works by Yeats

W.B. Yeats, *Collected Plays* (London: Macmillan, 1952)

W.B. Yeats, *Autobiographies*, ed. William H. O'Donnell and Douglas N. Archibald (New York: Scribner, 1999)

W.B. Yeats, *Explorations,* selected by Mrs W.B. Yeats (London: Macmillan, 1962)

W.B. Yeats, *A Vision* (London: Macmillan, 1962)

Biography

R.F. Foster, *W.B. Yeats. A Life*, 2 vols. (Oxford University Press, 2003)

Index of Titles and First Lines

ALMA CLASSICS

ALMA CLASSICS aims to publish mainstream and lesser-known European classics in an innovative and striking way, while employing the highest editorial and production standards. By way of a unique approach the range offers much more, both visually and textually, than readers have come to expect from contemporary classics publishing.

To order any of our titles and for up-to-date information about our current and forthcoming publications, please visit our website on:

www.almaclassics.com